A FALLIBLE CHURCH

A FALLIBLE CHURCH

Lambeth Essays

Edited by Kenneth Stevenson

DARTON·LONGMAN + TODD

First published in 2008 by
Darton, Longman and Todd Ltd
1 Spencer Court
140 – 142 Wandsworth High Street
London SW18 4JJ

ISBN-10: 0–232–52730–X
ISBN-13: 978–0–232–52730–8

Typeset by YHT Ltd, London
Printed in Great Britain by
Cromwell Press, Trowbridge, Wiltshire.

For Rowan,
friend,
colleague,
fellow pilgrim in the wound of knowledge

Contents

Preface

As Lambeth 2008 approaches, public speculation mounts over how many Anglican Provinces will take part, how world-wide Anglicanism can hold together, and whether there is indeed something Anglican that is worth sustaining. These essays are intended to show, to the contrary, how the Communion continues to work, how Anglican identity is very much alive and kicking, and how these insights could point to a more patient and humble future. The greatest moments of crisis in the past, whether in the fourth, the twelfth, or the sixteenth centuries, have invariably been theologically the most creative, however difficult they've been to live through – and there is no reason to think that the present will be otherwise, either for ourselves or for our many ecumenical partners.

It would be impossible for a collection of this sort to be somehow representative of the entire Communion. In the first part, the worked examples, the spotlight falls on the country where Anglicanism was born (England), and the continent where most Anglicans now live (Africa). The second part, concerning areas of unfinished business, is necessarily more wide-ranging.

If there is a unifying feature of these essays, it is a desire to pay far more attention to history and common narrative than many Anglicans – and others – are ready to give at the moment, and that extends especially to the work of earlier Lambeth Conferences, all too often forgotten. We simply cannot, as sometimes appears to be the case, be panicked into a situation which may be caricatured along the lines of 'this is all unprecedented' – 'we must do something' – 'there is nothing else on offer' – 'therefore we must do such-and-such, or else'! On the face of it, these essays may well offer some surprise facts, like the call for the Church of Sweden to be represented at the first Lambeth Conference in 1867, or the refusal of the Archbishop of York to attend, to say nothing of a recent Sudanese General Synod's decision, when provided with the opportunity to debate homo-sexuality, to move to next business, because there were other more important issues to deal with.

The desire to reawaken a sense of history and common narrative, however, goes far wider and deeper. We need to engage more positively and critically with the past. One area that deserves more scrutiny is the notion of covenant, which may have fine biblical roots, but which, when applied to the Church, became a far more slippery term at the Reforma-tion. Richard Hooker, for example, would only handle it with a very long pair of tongs, and by the middle of the seventeenth century, Jeremy Taylor strove hard to ensure a less restrictive interpretation than was held by many of his contemporaries. As one looks at the spread of Anglicanism in the period since, there are many signs of the ambiguity of the imperial past – slavery being an obvious and appalling example – yet there is far more to rejoice over, as God continues to use humanity, fallible cultural receptacles and all, for the furtherance of his kingdom. Our generation will make its own mistakes, of which future generations, as they make theirs, will doubtless pick over the details. Never-theless, we still need to be more positive about our conflicts, in which connection James Jones' account of a tripartite conversation between Akure (Nigeria), Virginia (ECUSA), and Liverpool (England) is a significant example.

Then there is unfinished business over Primacy. Here one begins to notice a shift from a functional view ('this is what I am supposed to do') to a more essential view ('this is what I am'). Hitherto, Anglicanism has enjoyed both trajectories in the three-fold order of deacon, presbyter, and bishop. But to load Primacy heavily with this extra burden is a new departure for us. This observation may explain some of the muddles we are getting into – though what we are facing in some areas could be a more directly 'leadership versus the led' scenario. Could this be another way of saying that we may be heading for a higher doctrine of 'Communion' than we can at present reasonably service?

An increasingly important companion to theology concerns ecclesiastical law. The notion of an already-nascent common law in the Communion, emerging from each Province's own history and collective discipline, is strenuously documented by Norman Doe, a common law which could well be upset by pressure for central control of any kind. This essay, along with John Gladwin's, is based on papers delivered at the Conference of the Ecclesiastical Law Society, held in Liverpool, January 2007, and reproduced with permission.

As all these essays demonstrate, history and common narrative should not become arguments for a Eurocentric standpoint, nor should they be excuses for an 'anything goes' pragmatism. One of my abiding memories of Lambeth 1998 was the Filipino Eucharist, which began with the ringing of a gong, which silenced everyone, and was then sounded louder and louder as the liturgy moved into the opening song. In thanking my fellow essayists for generously collaborating in this small contribution to what is sometimes called 'occasional theology', I hope that the result may serve in some measure to hush the strife, and awaken to a deeper and more tolerant discipleship an Anglican Communion which has been blessed by God with far more life and vitality than we are often aware of. It is not for nothing that the epistle-reading often used at episcopal consecrations in England should be that unforgettable passage from Paul's Second Letter to the Corinthians that includes the image of clay jars (2 Corinthians 4:7). As any archaeologist knows, such material has remarkable gifts of survival – but it needs handling with care when in actual living use!

Kenneth Stevenson
Bishopsgrove
Fareham
Commemoration of William Wilberforce,
Social Reformer (+1833)
30th July 2007

Contributors

Kenneth Stevenson is Bishop of Portsmouth

John Gladwin is Bishop of Chelmsford

Terry Louden is Vicar of East Meon and Langrish, and Honorary Canon of Portsmouth

David Stancliffe is Bishop of Salisbury

James Jones is Bishop of Liverpool

Graham James is Bishop of Norwich

Norman Doe is Director of the Centre for Law and Religion, Cardiff University

Mark Chapman is Vice-Principal of Ripon College, Cuddesdon

PART ONE

Worked Examples

1

John Gladwin

The Local and the Universal and the Meaning of Anglicanism: Kenya

The Anglican Settlement

I was brought up to believe that the Reformation, among other things, achieved four things for the Church of England. First, it affirmed the primary authority of the Scriptures as God's word leading us to Jesus Christ. This is the text that gives the Gospel to us. Second, it restricted the credal foundation of the church to the historic creeds, as set out in the 39 Articles of Religion. These together with the Book of Common Prayer and the Ordinal defined the doctrinal and ecclesial character of the Church of England. Not all the Councils of the Early Church were accepted as carrying authority within the life of the church. Third, by a variety of historical incidents and the English rejection of the Puritan demand for further reform, the Church of England held on to the historic shape of its three-fold ministry. Fourth, it removed the power of the Bishop of Rome over the church, thereby emphasising the local character of the government of the church. All these characteristics of the church have endured and help define the Anglican inheritance. The Chicago/Lambeth Quadrilateral in the twentieth century is formed in this classic Anglican manner. These four simply stated boundaries of that Statement define Anglicanism in its international form.

This is how the Windsor Report puts it:

... as inherent parts of this sacred deposit, and therefore essential to the restoration of unity among the divided branches of Christendom, we account the following, to wit:

a. The Holy Scriptures of the Old and New Testaments as the revealed Word of God.
b. The Nicene Creed as the sufficient statement of the Christian Faith.
c. The two Sacraments, Baptism and the Supper of the Lord, ministered with unfailing use of Christ's words of institution and the elements ordained by him.
d. The Historic Episcopate, locally adapted in the methods of its administration to the varying needs of the nations and peoples called of God into the unity of His Church.[1]

That is it!

To be in full communion with Anglican churches, local churches have to evidence these marks within their life and order. It is interesting to note that the Chicago/Lambeth Quadrilateral is a short and very flexible document. It defines the Scriptures and their authority but not how they are to be interpreted beyond faithfulness to the Nicene Creed. It does not set out any particular model for the historic episcopate. So within these boundaries churches may order their lives and affairs and their pastoral oversight as they think fit. Thus, on a whole variety of matters churches within the Anglican family have different disciplines and practices. These include women and holy orders, orders affecting marriage and family life, and the size, authority, and power of dioceses and their bishops. A core set of commitments making us identifiably Anglican allow a great diversity of experience in the local church. The Church of England is itself a demonstration of this truth in the variety of histories and traditions in our 44 dioceses.

Both in terms of law and doctrine we have resisted the route of maximal defining statements. We are neither bound by the books of Catholic Dogma nor the fulsome Calvinist Westminster Confession. The Church of England's Canon Law is bound in a small and basic document which when read carefully gives those under canonical oaths of obedience plenty of room for choice. If we then ask the question as to the nature of the local church we have to consider, within Anglicanism, a variety of levels of life. We now have the Anglican Communion. But that is a gathering of the Provinces of the Communion with no power of governance vested in it. We have the regular meeting of the Primates. This has no constitutional structure. It is a gathering of people in their shared role. Of longer endurance we have the Lambeth Conference which, again, has no juridical authority but is a recognition of the pivotal nature of Episcopal ministry within our tradition. Resolutions of this conference have moral but not governmental authority. Provinces and/or national churches may well have crucial structures for the governance of the church but even these have to recognise the Episcopal order of the church. That leads to our understanding that the diocese is the basic form of the local church. As we know, in the variety of experience across the Communion, that can take many forms. Dioceses and their bishops can be very powerful and directive agencies, or they can work in a highly devolved manner through parishes and the church in its immediate locality. In England we tend to have large dioceses, giving a great deal of scope to the parishes and the church within them. In places like Nigeria many dioceses are hardly any larger than English deaneries and the bishop may carry a great deal of immediate authority over them.

It is this sense of our history that shapes the way I approach the present challenges within Anglicanism. We need to exercise great care and not a little caution in looking at ways forward for us all. There are real dangers to our character and inheritance in trying to resolve our problems by new definitions of faith that seek to close down debate and the capacity of local churches to carry forward the mission of Christ within their own context. We should be very cautious of any proposal for new structures of power within the wider Communion drifting us in the Roman and pontifical direction. The moral and pastoral authority of statements made by the bishops of the Communion or by the Primates is much more important than any legal and disciplinary authority attached to them.

Kenya

There are two examples from my experience of visiting our partners in the Church of the Province of Kenya last year. These have much to teach us. Indeed, we all have much to learn from one another. The stereotyping of different parts of the Communion is both untruthful and unhelpful. Africa is not made up of old-fashioned and reactionary churches struggling to catch up with the enlightened wisdom of the northern and western churches. The northern and western churches are not cesspits of rational unbelief and moral disorder. Every church, in the proper continuity of Anglican life, is working hard at making sense of the meaning of the Gospel within its cultural and social setting. All face challenges and all have real problems.

It is well known that when it was made public that I had agreed to become a patron of Changing Attitude, the Archbishop of Kenya issued a direction that our visit should come to an end. We did eventually sort this out and the visit was completed with the Archbishop's office agreement and help. The Archbishop did, however, indicate that he would raise the issue at the Provincial Council a few weeks later. I understand that this did come on the agenda. The bishops of the four dioceses with which Chelmsford has a historic link made it clear that the matter belonged within the jurisdiction of the dioceses not of the Province. That carried the day. Links are therefore established primarily between dioceses. That underlined the character of the Kenyan Church whose constitution works on a strong diocesan model. There is a bottom-up sense to its history and governance – the Province being a gathering of the dioceses to ensure good governance for the church. The bishop within the diocese is the focal point of authority and for the pursuit of the mission of the church.

The second interesting experience from our visit to Kenya gave me a much deeper sense of how much we can learn from one another. In the midst of the public controversy surrounding our visit – at its height – we were in the Diocese of Kirinyaga in the Samburu region. This flat land beyond Mount Kenya, which you can see on a good day in the distance, is suffering severe drought. Meeting its nomadic village people and sharing in the ministry of confirmation with them was one of the most moving experiences of my life. One of our groups of curates spent some extra time visiting these villages. They had to come to terms with the presence of polygamy within Christian villages.

It so happened that at the same time as these encounters were making our people think again, I was meeting Archbishop David Gitari, the former Primate and a very courageous leader of the Church in East Africa, who gave us an insight into the character of the Kenyan Church. He also gave me a copy of his latest book on 'Responsible Church Leadership'. In this book I learnt about the Kenyan Church's journey of pastoral theology in relation to the question of polygamy. It is clear that Archbishop Gitari believes that the resolution of the 1888 Lambeth Conference forbidding the baptism of people in polygamous relationships is a piece of imperialism by a church which was then dominated by white English bishops. Let me quote to you a paragraph of what he says:

Godly discernment is needed to determine which customs, though not ideally Christian, are nevertheless tolerable to the gospel. The criteria of the tolerable customs are that: there is no clear teaching against it in the scriptures; and that it is likely to die a natural death when the Christian church is firmly established. In one case, of great importance for Africa, the Anglican Church has failed to recognise a tolerable custom. 1988 was the centenary of the Lambeth Conference's decisive, and I believe mistaken, refusal of baptism to polygamists. The issue of polygamy meets our suggested criteria: the New Testament contains no implicit or explicit statement on

polygamy, unless it is Paul's instruction that bishops and
deacons should be married to one wife (1 Timothy 3:2,
12). However, polygamist men who want to become
Christians have been handled as if their condition were
intolerable to the gospel.[2]

The Archbishop goes on to a long discussion of the issue
and then sets before us the measures adopted by the
Anglican Church of Kenya in 1982. I will not list them but
suffice it to say they do not conform to the 1888 Resolution
of the Lambeth Conference. Local needs being met by a
careful process of theological and pastoral discernment for
the sake of the mission of the Gospel. The Archbishop was
manifestly disappointed that the Lambeth Conference did
not revoke its 1888 Resolutions. He did not, however, see
the Kenyan Church as bound by them.

It is clear that the Kenyan Church looks to the international gatherings and instruments of the Communion to
provide a forum of assistance in which a great deal of
mutual listening happens. They are not looking for the
wider church to control or direct their decisions but to
hear, to discern in a theological manner, and receive them.
The issues facing us today, though different, are not a
thousand miles from this sort of pastoral challenge. If the
Communion is to work it needs to be a place where
churches, holding within the boundaries of the Chicago/
Lambeth Quadrilateral, can without threat share their different challenges and journeys and find help and encouragement. The Kenyan story has much to teach all of us.
Dare one say that we might also learn some important
things by listening carefully to the pastoral and theological
experience of our brothers and sisters in North America?
The message is that Resolutions of the Lambeth

Conference have not always been good news for the mission
of the Gospel across our very diverse world. That is why,
after the 1998 Conference and having observed the 1988
Conference, I came to the conclusion that Lambeth Conferences have been too dominated by the political process of
passing resolutions and not enough by the offering of pastoral and theological support, advice, and comment to the
churches of the Communion and to our wider ecumenical
friends. All of that is rooted in an understanding of our
Anglican tradition of ecclesial order. We take the local
church very seriously as at the heart of our order. In an
international and global world we need to be careful not to
undermine this vital character of our identity.

Some Questions

The Anglican order may, therefore, have something rather
crucial to contribute in the modern world. This is about
how we maintain communion across difference in an
international world without compromising the pivotal significance of the local. The last quarter of the twentieth
century witnessed a huge shift into global experience.
Contemporary systems of communication and the workings
of a global and liberalised economy mean that we are all
utterly interconnected. We cannot conduct our affairs as if
we can cocoon ourselves from the wider human community. In even more recent times, we have become all too
aware of our total interdependent nature when thinking of
the issues of the future of the planet – global warming and
the stewardship of creation. So we need each other and we
need to be in real relationship.

What we are not succeeding in is the nurturing of the
vitality and self-worth of the local in the face of the growing

power of the international. There are struggles around institutions like the structure of the World Bank and real concerns about the weakness of the global south within it. There are proper concerns about the way both northern and Asian economies are developing and having a destructive effect upon the future of the planet and upon the capacity of smaller developing nations to become genuinely self-governing. In Christian Aid we watch the impact of the systems of the global economy on small and highly vulnerable local communities. Often we see local communities unable to sustain their own chosen and needed patterns of life in the face of the power of our global order. We cannot live as if this process of globalisation has not happened and we must not let it ride roughshod over local autonomy and the choices of ordinary people and their communities.

The twentieth century has seen a massive movement in which power centralises, and with it the growth of powerful states and powerful corporate institutions both of a public and a private character. That is not to suggest that these are of themselves evil and corrupt. Many have the highest standards and values. But it does suggest that the way things work in the relationship between the large and global institutions and the small and local organisations and communities brings constant pressure on the local. The issues we face in the UK and elsewhere in western economies concerning the impact of ever-growing retail giants – Tesco, Sainsbury's, Morrison's, and Asda in the UK – on the wider retail market, are embedded in the challenges facing the international order. Is the genuinely local being squeezed by the operations of the international economic order?

We have yet to find answers to all of this. Part of the

problem is that we are operating in a new global environment with old post-war-shaped institutions that were
established when the need was to order and control. Now
the need is to build relationships and enable diversity and
flexibility to flourish. What we must not do in the Anglican
Communion is to find twentieth-century structural solutions to twenty-first-century challenges. We too need to
enable diversity within flourishing relationships. That does
mean taking the local and the diocese with much greater
seriousness than some of our conversations suggest. It also
means that we need to use the opportunities of our global
relationships to listen carefully to one another about how
our interrelated world is affecting all of us and how we can
better exercise our responsibility towards one another.
Thus the agenda centres on the movement of our culture at
the foundation of our mission rather than the presenting
issues on the surface. The task is to create a process of
mutual support rather than one of enforcing an outmoded
conformity.

What we have in the Anglican Communion is a model of
how on a large and diverse field you put down the boundary
markers:

- Bible
- Nicene Creed
- Gospel sacraments
- The three-fold ministry of bishop, priest, and deacon.

On that playing field self-governing churches can inhabit
their own space and at the same time engage with one
another. They may need instruments to enable this process
of mutuality and a common inheritance. These can change
as the needs change. The Windsor Report clearly sees the

need for changes in the structure and processes of the Communion. This needs to build on an ever-evolving history. So we have seen the development of the Lambeth Conference, the ACC, and the Primates' Meeting. These are not institutions of governance. They are instruments to enable mutual engagement and shared experience. They should also be places that enable the churches to work through moments of conflict and difference on the basis of their living within the borders as agreed. We have quite a good record in these matters, as is evidenced by the way the question of women and the episcopate has been handled. The autonomy of churches has been respected, enabling the development of the ordained ministry of women without imposing it upon churches against their will. Churches must make their own decisions and these have to be mutually respected, provided they do not breach the boundaries established and a sense of mutual obligation.

In other words, the process of change within the Communion needs to strengthen the life of the local church and enable the communion of churches to flourish in the context of this rich history and diversity.

Conclusion

In summary, the task must remain essentially Anglican in culture. That means building relationships rather than institutions. We should be very cautious about any solution to difference that seeks to give power to institutions and gives up on the patient work of nurturing relationships and keeping conversation alive and well. The same truth applies to statements of faith. We have rather a lot of them in the history of the church. In one sense their existence is evidence of a failure in communion and in conflict resolution.

An Anglican Covenant could be seen in that light. We resort to words as a way of settling difference. If the words capture the essential communion we all share they help us move forward together. If they exclude, they further divide the church. We will need to exercise real caution here. To use another phrase of Archbishop Gitari, we must never allow the urgent to take us away from the important.[3] Exploring relationships and building communion takes time and requires patience. In a culture dominated by the immediate, we need to watch lest we rush to solutions which later the church will regret.

Let me give an image of the significance of all of this – an encouraging snapshot of what diversity means for us. A friend found himself worshipping in one of the most conservative and traditional catholic parishes in ECUSA. The church is opposed to the ordained ministry of women. It has not, however, broken its communion with its bishop. The service includes baptism. The baptism includes baptism of the adopted children of same-sex couples. No one thinks there is anything unusual or unorthodox in a same-sex couple bringing their adopted child for baptism. That is diversity and difference at work. Dividing the church up into 'conservative' and 'liberal' factions fails to understand what is really happening at a time when human life is beginning to learn to accept and then enjoy its diversity.

Bishop Tom Butler put the challenge well in his Presidential address to his Diocesan Synod in March 2007. Responding to the demand of the Anglican Primates' Meeting in Tanzania earlier in 2007 he comments:

And here I believe lies the fundamental flaw. The Primates have misunderstood the nature of our communion. From the consecration of the first overseas Anglican bishops there was no intention of creating a kind of soviet bloc Communion where each province had to march in step with one another. Listen to this letter of the English Bishops to the Philadelphia Convention in 1786 when they had been requested to consecrate an American priest as bishop. They wrote: 'We cannot but be extremely cautious, lest we should be instruments of establishing an ecclesiastical system which will be called a branch of the Church of England, but afterwards may possibly appear to have departed from it essentially, either in doctrine or discipline.'

There was no intention of creating a branch of the Church of England in America ... I would like us to return to our roots and ask ourselves, is it our calling to be a Communion where we must march in step and if one province departs from the others in doctrine or discipline, they must depart from the Communion? ... Or is it our calling to be a Commonwealth of Anglican provinces, uncompromised by the beliefs and behaviours of other provinces, trusting that they know what is best for the Church and world in their particular culture with their particular history and tradition? I don't hear that argument being made. Perhaps it should.[4]

Either we rejoice in our Anglican inheritance or we slump back into these centralising universals that belong to an age that, for the moment, has passed. The twenty-first century needs something different from us.

Notes

1 *The Lambeth Commission on Communion, the Windsor Report 2004* (London: The Anglican Communion Office, 2004), p.90.
2 David M. Gitari, *Responsible Church Leadership* (Nairobi Acton Publishers, 2005), p.110.
3 Op. cit., p.i.
4 Address made by the Bishop of Southwark to his Diocesan Synod, 10 March 2007.

2

Terry Louden

Ghana and Portsmouth: a view from Cape Coast

IDWAL

In 1963, in the light of world-wide and pan-Anglican discussions about mutual responsibility and interdependence, the Diocese of Guildford established a link of friendship and support with the Anglican Church in Nigeria. Fourteen years later, in 1977, Guildford persuaded its geographical neighbours in the Dioceses of Chichester and Portsmouth to extend the link to cover other countries in West Africa with an Anglican tradition. The link was inaugurated in Portsmouth with 'West Africa Way', a procession of witness from the city's Guildhall to the Anglican Cathedral in July 1978. Thus was born what is known as IDWAL (Inter Diocesan West Africa Link). It remains the only such organisation within the Anglican Communion through which an adjacent group of dioceses within one Province is linked with a particular geographical region of the Anglican world.

From a UK point of view it is easy to make too much of this, and to imagine that our inter-diocesan relationships in

England are replicated across national borders and provincial boundaries in West Africa. The Anglican Churches in Gambia, Sierra Leone, Liberia, Guinea, Ghana, Nigeria, and Cameroon have little in common apart from an identity formed by their common heritage. What geographical unity might once have existed between those countries has been radically disturbed by recent historical and political events. The decades since independence have been times of uncertainty and, often, despair. Though West Africa presently has recovered some stability and peace, the last forty years have witnessed civil wars, social upheaval, and death and destruction, especially in Nigeria, Sierra Leone, and Liberia, and a succession of military coups and repressive regimes elsewhere.

The way in which the IDWAL link operates from the UK has changed over the thirty years of its life. For many years there was a definite structure, with an elected and appointed inter-diocesan committee. Following reviews in 1998 and 2005, the structures are much looser, and contact and working together depends on the good relationships between the episcopally appointed IDWAL officers in the three constituent dioceses. In 1998, the geographical focus of the English dioceses was changed to its present format. Currently, Guildford's links remain with Nigeria, though the Anglican Church there is growing at such a pace that the links with Guildford are consequently uneven. Chichester has links with Sierra Leone, Guinea, and Cameroon, and is developing contacts in Liberia. Portsmouth's relationships are now primarily, though not exclusively, with the nine dioceses in Ghana, which are part of the Province of West Africa. Though West Africa, including Nigeria, is a huge and diverse region, in Anglican circles the IDWAL acronym is still recognised and respected, as a symbol of companionship in the Gospel both within West Africa and with the three dioceses in England. The IDWAL logo is on the home page of the Province of Nigeria's website.

Since 1998, some forty links have been established between parishes and schools in the Diocese of Portsmouth and Anglican churches in Ghana. The aim of these companion links is encouragement in the Christian faith and mission, learning about different societies and cultures, friendship, and mutual support. The links are sustained by prayer, by letter, by phone and email, and by personal visits. Experience has shown that links come alive as Christians from the UK and Ghana visit each other. The diocesan bishop has directed Lent Appeal funds to support a new library building at St Nicholas Anglican Seminary, Cape Coast and to help with the foundation of an Anglican tertiary college, and the Portsmouth IDWAL committee has been able to provide and to install computers in diocesan offices in Ghana.

Links have been set up largely on a deanery to diocese basis. This was a convenient arrangement, since Portsmouth has eight deaneries and Ghana now has nine dioceses, though only seven when the deanery–diocese relationship was established. The Deanery of Petersfield, for example, is linked with the Anglican Diocese of Cape Coast, where the first resident Church of England presence in West Africa was located.

The city of Cape Coast is today the capital and administrative centre of the Central Region of Ghana. It is situated on the coast, as its name implies, just under a hundred miles west of Accra, the capital city. At the last census in 2000, Cape Coast had a population of some 80,000 people, and it has grown since, so it is a town or city of considerable size. Its economy depends on fishing, the marketing of

locally grown fruit and vegetables and, increasingly, tourism. It is a university city. Its most famous contemporary
son is Michael Essien, the Chelsea and Ghana footballer,
who attended school there.

European traders first visited that part of the West African coast in the sixteenth century. In those days it was a
difficult and dangerous coast for ships, because of the lack
of natural harbours and the presence of strong currents. So
wherever a sheltered, accessible beach could be found, the
Europeans competed with one another for control. For a
hundred years or more, from 1555 to 1664, this small strip
of beach was fought over by the English, Portuguese,
Dutch, Danes, and Swedes. The Portuguese built the first
trade lodge in 1555, and gave the area its name. They called
it 'Cabo Corso', meaning short cape. Later on this became
corrupted to the anglicised 'Cape Coast'.

From 1664, Cape Coast was permanently in British
hands, and remained the administrative centre of what was
then called the 'Gold Coast' until 1877, when the capital
was moved to Accra. From that time Cape Coast became
an important centre of the British arm of the transatlantic
slave trade. Indeed, the castle that was built on the beach
was described in 1837 by the then Governor Maclean as
having been, until 1807, the 'grand emporium of the British
slave trade'.[1]

Through the course of 2007, the 200th anniversary year
of the legislation abolishing the trade in British ships, the
history of the Atlantic slave trade has been recounted in
books and films, radio and television programmes, displays
and exhibitions. Cape Coast was a significant African outlet
for the trade, one of the ports from which the infamous
'Middle Passage' began. Of the estimated eleven million
Africans transported over a period of some four hundred

years, some three million were carried in British ships. In the 1790s, the decade when the trade was at its height, a ship left a British port on the first leg of the triangular trade every second day. At that time, Britain was the leading European nation in the trade, and Cape Coast its main centre in West Africa. The ancestors of hundreds of thousands of people living today in the English-speaking Caribbean, the United States, and many other countries passed through the 'door of no return' in Cape Coast Castle. Today, the castle, extended and remodelled in Victorian times, is a World Heritage Site, a well-preserved historical museum. To take the tour, and to visit the dungeons and to see the 'door of no return' is a moving and chilling experience.

In the eighteenth century, while the slaves were being held, hundreds at a time, in the castle dungeons, in unspeakable conditions, husbands separated from wives, women abused by the guards, waiting for the next ship to anchor offshore, within the same castle walls Christian worship was being offered to Almighty God. Chaplains – clergy of the Church of England – are recorded as being present in Cape Coast Castle from 1697, in order to meet the spiritual and pastoral needs of the British who were living there as the military and commercial representatives of the Royal African Company. As well as leading Sunday worship, clergy were required for funerals, which were frequent, as disease took its toll. So were baptisms, as relationships with local women became a recognised aspect of life, irrespective of whether there was a wife back at home.

A significant development took place in 1751, when the Revd Thomas Thompson, who had for five years been a missionary for the Society for the Propagation of the Gospel

(SPG – as it was then called) in the American colony of New Jersey, offered to go to the Gold Coast to work, not just with the expatriates, but also among the Africans – some of whom he had come to know in America – in their original home. Thompson had a vision of mission beyond chaplaincy, reaching out beyond the castle walls. He spent only five years in Cape Coast, and the results of his missionary work were limited. But he did realise that the high mortality rate among white Christian missionaries could best be addressed by training indigenous people to undertake the work. So he sent three African boys, all under the age of twelve, to England for education. Two died, but one, Philip Quaque, survived. In 1765, Philip Quaque became the first African to be ordained in the Church of England, and on his return to Cape Coast the following year, the first African to serve as a Anglican priest in sub-Saharan Africa. He spent the next fifty years in Cape Coast, until his death in 1816, as 'missionary, school-master, and catechist to the Negroes on the Gold Coast',[2] as well as being chaplain to the castle.

We know something of the attitudes of Thompson to the slave trade. In 1772, he published a book about it, dedicated to the English merchants and investors who financed the trade. In *The African Trade for Negro Slaves Shown to be Consistent with the Principles of Humanity and with the Laws of Revealed Religion*, Thompson assured his readers that the trade had full biblical, Christian, and ecclesiastical endorsement. He argued that the Scriptures regarded slavery as normative. Leviticus commanded the enslavement of conquered people. Even in the time of Jesus slavery was endemic, and he appears to have accepted it. Thompson even proposed that it was in the slaves' best interests to be transported, as they would have a better life. Of course, he was writing for a London audience at a time when the abolitionists were beginning the campaign to end the trade (Mansfield's judgement about the illegality of slavery in Britain was given in 1772) and the pro-slavers needed to have their own intellectual and moral justification. There is some evidence that British attitudes in Cape Coast were not so clear cut. Thompson admitted that he had known men long involved in the trade who 'could never well reconcile themselves to it'. Even his own conscience was uneasy. There was something disagreeable in the notion of human beings, 'even the lowest of such, being treated like mere beasts or cattle'.[3]

We know of Quaque's ministry in Cape Coast after his return from London. We do not know for certain of his attitudes to the slave trade. We do know that John Moore, the clergyman with whom he lodged and who instructed him in London, was the son of a pro-slavery Archbishop of Canterbury, who judged the trade as a legitimate and honourable occupation for a Christian gentleman. Quaque's education in London made him, to some extent, part of the establishment. On the other hand, back in Cape Coast, there was some racism directed at him, and it seems that apart from baptisms, weddings, and funerals, he held services in the castle infrequently. Governor Brew told Quaque that he would never 'sit under the nose of a black boy to hear him pointing or laying out their faults'.[4]

Throughout Quaque's long ministry of half a century it seems that a communion service was never held in the castle. Of course, Church of England practice in the late eighteenth century was for infrequent communion, perhaps only monthly or even quarterly, but even at Easter the sacrament was not celebrated in the castle. The reason for this does not seem to have been to do with the colour of

Quaque's skin, or a refusal to accept his ministry. The Christians in the castle felt that, as slave traders and because of the nature of their work, they could not, in good conscience, attend. Quaque explained this in a letter to SPG in London saying that no one was willing to 'embrace the Rapture of the Lord's Supper, and the only plea they offer is that while they are here acting against Light and Conscience they dare not come to that holy Table'.[5] Quaque did celebrate the Holy Communion with his own family, and occasionally with the sick or dying.

We also know that the wife he married in England died soon after arriving in Cape Coast, whereupon Quaque married his late wife's maid. Not only did he marry her but, unusually and irregularly, he performed the public ceremony himself, no other clergyman being available. In his last years there is evidence of loss of faith, and a return to the religion of his African ancestors. Nevertheless, both Quaque and Thompson are still regarded with esteem and honour in the Anglican Church in Ghana, as the pioneers and founders of Anglican mission there. Each has a church named after him in Cape Coast today.

Some three years ago, sitting outside Cape Coast Castle, I remember asking a Ghanaian priest how the Ghana of today regards the slave trade, and how the Wilberforce anniversary would be marked in Ghana in 2007. I was slightly surprised by the lack of passion in the answer I received. Basically, his opinion was that this had all happened long ago, that Africans as well as Europeans had been involved, and that the experience of the past had little bearing on the pressing problems and issues of today. The abolition of the trade was marked in Ghana in 2007, though it was rather overshadowed by the fiftieth anniversary of Ghana's independence from Britain, an anniversary which

occurred in the same month of March. There were ceremonies and services in Cape Coast and in Elmina, the
oldest of all the slave forts, ten miles west along the coast.
BBC Radio 4 broadcast a Sunday morning service from St
James's Anglican Church in Elmina. However, it remains
true that the sad history of the trade will always mean more
to the descendants of those transported than it will to those
whose ancestors never left Africa, some of whom may have
been complicit in the trade themselves. The anniversary
gave a stimulus to tourism, with the makeover of buildings,
and the opening of new exhibitions and memorials, like the
one in Assin Manso, forty miles north of Cape Coast, where
the captured slaves, brought from many different areas,
were gathered together for the final march to the coast.
Furthermore, not every person of African descent wishes to
regard himself or herself as part of the African diaspora.
However strong the feelings of white English Christians for
the need for a public apology for slavery, and however
contrite modern African leaders are for African complicity,
places like Cape Coast Castle are never likely to be a kind of
Auschwitz – a place of pilgrimage for the African holocaust.
Two centuries have passed, and both Ghanaians and
members of the diaspora are properly most focussed on the
present and the immediate future. Cape Coast Castle
stands as an important site of historical heritage and a place
of learning and reflection about slavery, but it is not a
memorial.

In that sense, the past is past. And yet, in another way, it
is not. For in the Anglican Church in Ghana today, there
remain aspects of cultural and religious dependence which
are very much the consequences of the colonial and
imperial relationship between England and Ghana.

Canon John Pobee, a contemporary Ghanaian Anglican,

writes that 'after Quaque, nothing much of significance happened in the Gold Coast in terms of Anglicanism'.[6] This was certainly true throughout the nineteenth century. Chaplains served the colonial administration, and that was about it. How, then, has the current Anglican Church in Ghana, with its nine dioceses, developed over the past hundred years, and what is its ethos and character?

The Church, which had been, in the eighteenth and early nineteenth century, the adjunct of trade, including the slave trade, became in the early twentieth century the partner of the British colonial administration. Supported and largely financed by SPG, what came into being on the Gold Coast, as in other parts of the British Empire, was effectively a branch of the Church of England overseas. The Church was actually known as the 'English Church Mission' right up until the 1950s. In the local vernacular it was known as *aban-mu-asor*, the Church in the Castle. The first bishop, Nathaniel Hamlyn, was consecrated in 1904. Episcopal leadership remained in the hands of expatriates until after Ghana gained political independence in 1957; Bishop Lemaire, the first African, was consecrated in 1968. Thereafter a network of dioceses slowly took shape across the country. A second diocese, Kumasi, was created in 1973; four more – Cape Coast, Sekondi, Koforidua, and Sunyani in 1981. A seventh, Tamale, was born in 1997, and an eighth, Ho, in 2003. With the division of the diocese of Sekondi into two parts in 2006, the new diocese of Wiawso is the ninth in Ghana. As this diocesan structure took shape, so a synodical structure emerged alongside. The Anglican Church in Ghana is part of the Anglican Province of West Africa, formed in 1951, which also includes Gambia, Guinea, Sierra Leone, Liberia, and the missionary diocese of Cameroon, but not, of course,

Nigeria, which became a separate Province in 1979. Within the Anglican Church in Ghana, dioceses are relatively independent one from another. Since 1982, there has existed a body called the Joint Anglican Diocesan Council, on which the bishops and other diocesan representatives sit, and which meets once or twice a year, but whose deliberations are purely advisory. The JADC was long ago tasked with trying to bring clergy salaries across Ghana into line with one another, but has not succeeded in doing this. Part of our Church of England legacy seems to have been a strong sense of diocesan identity, but little incentive for inter-diocesan co-operation.

The Anglican Church in Ghana was formed in the High Church, Anglo-Catholic tradition, due to the influence of SPG. In other parts of West Africa, Nigeria and Sierra Leone, for example, the Anglican Church has more of a Low Church, Evangelical character, precisely because the evangelical Church Missionary Society (as it was then called) was the driving force instead of USPG (as it became in 1965). In Ghana, as elsewhere, the Church's particular history has given it particular characteristics.

The original expatriate bishops were active, determined, committed, and self-sacrificing. But they came from an ecclesiological tradition which was authoritarian, and they were also working in partnership with the colonial power. Thus a rather dictatorial tradition of episcopacy was established that had no mechanism for self-criticism, or for effective and consistent listening to the needs of the community of faith. When invited to consider setting up a formal, written constitution for the Diocese of Accra in the inter-war years Bishop Aglionby replied: 'the bishop is the constitution'.[7] So a top-down model of ecclesiastical management was set up, and there remains evidence of this tradition in the current relationships between bishops, priests, and people in Ghana today. Bishops are treated with a respect and honour that is to be admired or with a deference and a formality that is to be questioned, according to your point of view.

The more democratic models of government which the Church of England has adopted since 1969 have not yet been properly adapted to the Ghanaian context, if indeed it is right that they should be. Synods do meet at diocesan level maybe once a year, but decision-making processes are not often clear. The English parliamentary model on which the synodical system is based is probably unsuitable in the longer term. The Provincial Synod meets very irregularly, because of cost, distance, and, in recent years, the impossibility of travel due to political strife and violence. It is unclear what authority this meeting can effectively have. Decisions about the propriety of the ordination of women, for instance, are being taken at diocesan, rather than at provincial, level.

With the expatriate bishops came also a certain liturgical style, including a devotion to English forms of service, either the Book of Common Prayer or English Missal, English hymnody, Merbecke, acolytes and processions, servers and incense. Furthermore, this liturgical style was introduced as a tradition in such a way as to make it antipathetic to change rather than as part of a process of organic development.

If you attend a Sunday Eucharist in Ghana today you will encounter a curious and confusing mixture of styles. On Trinity Sunday, for instance, it is very reassuring to be able to sing Reginald Heber's words 'Holy, holy, holy, Lord God Almighty' to Dykes's well-known tune 'Nicaea', surrounded by men and women in 'English' choir dress, and by servers in cassock and cotta. The English visitor feels at home, or at least has a warm sense of nostalgia for what used to be. But this is surely inappropriate. Archbishop Rowan Williams said some time ago that the worst thing the Church of England ever did was to export *Hymns Ancient and Modern*. Churches in Ghana, obviously for cost reasons, tend still to use *Ancient and Modern Standard*, the version published in 1924. Ghana has a vibrant musical tradition, and choruses and songs from the local culture form part of the liturgy. But these, even in churches with progressive priests and congregations, tend to take second place to hymns written in and for the English context, especially in churches where English is well understood. Common Worship services are being used in some churches, but there remains a devotion to the Book of Common Prayer, especially among older clergy, and even to the Alternative Services Book 1980, which at least two dioceses still use regularly. There is also something of an expectation that the services personally favoured by the diocesan bishop will be used in the churches of the diocese. But why should forms of worship produced primarily for the Church of England be the norm?

The Anglican Church in Ghana is still in a relationship of cultural imbalance with regard to its English ancestor. The English Church has bequeathed a liturgical heritage which is rich, colourful, and comprehensive, but which does not travel well. In the Church of England we are accused of maintaining a worshipping tradition that is both too wordy and which requires too much literary skill. That does not transfer well to cultures where many people cannot read and where many languages are spoken. Christianity in Ghana is competitive and the Anglican Church in Ghana is numerically small. Of Ghana's population of 20 million, some 65 per cent profess the Christian faith. The Anglican Church in Ghana probably numbers no more than 100,000 people; there are approximately 2 million Catholics. The Methodist, Presbyterian, and Pentecostal Churches are numerically stronger than the Anglican Church. The Islamic tradition is strong, especially in the north. Members often give as their reason for leaving the Anglican Church the fact that the style and ceremonies of worship do not relate to their own culture and everyday life, and reflect too much of a foreign, rather than an indigenous tradition.

The question facing the Anglican Church in Ghana today is what it means to be an 'African Anglican'. What are the essential features of the Anglican tradition that the colonial era has bequeathed? What is secondary and can be abandoned? And how can those elements of church life and tradition that must be preserved be translated and incorporated into the various cultures which make up modern Ghana? The survival of what is a relatively weak church in terms of numbers and resources probably hinges on effective answers. Only African Anglicans can properly address these questions, but part of our responsibility, through our IDWAL links and partnerships, is to help in this process as listeners and friends. In so doing, we might ourselves discover more of what the essence of Anglicanism is.

The original principles for establishing successful indigenous churches were that they must aim to be self-governing, self-propagating, and self-supporting. The Anglican Church in Ghana is autonomous and self-governing, within the network of the Province and the Communion.

Self-propagating is to do with relating to the cultural context. Far-sighted church leaders in Ghana know how much work still needs to be done in this area. The Anglican Church in Ghana is having to live down its reputation as the religion of the colonial power prior to independence, and of the educated elite since. This presents particular problems for mission. One key to mission might well be what Canon Pobee calls the 'vernacular paradigm'. This involves not only translating the liturgy into local language and dialect, but also using local idiom, and less propositional and didactic forms of Christian teaching and expression. The role of indigenous music must increase. Corporate worship must enable people to feel at home in their own culture.

Lay involvement in mission is also developing. Given the emphasis on episcopacy in Ghana, it is not surprising that the local manifestations of church have been very clergy-centred. There has been the peculiar African creation of the 'catechist', 'the unsung hero of African church history. He was often a teacher or lesser mortal who prepared the ground for the missionary or priest, nursed the congregation, won souls for the church, and stayed with the poor at the grassroots. He was the holy man on whom the Christian community was focussed.'[8] The local catechist has an important part to play in church growth in Ghana, especially in outstations in rural areas which priests can visit only occasionally. But the catechists have been under-resourced in the past, and the training they have received has been inadequate. Dioceses are beginning to address this.

Then there is the role of women. In the Anglican Church in Ghana, women play a fundamental role in lay church life through the Mothers Union and the Fellowship of the Good Shepherd, but this is often expressed only in practical ways. Their contribution to the insights of faith, and the opportunities they should have for leadership are only now beginning to be recognised. In August 2007, the first two women students began training for ordination at the Anglican seminary of St Nicholas, in Cape Coast.

And there is the financial issue. The Anglican Church in Ghana is not properly self-supporting. Some dioceses, though not all, can just about, though not always, pay their clergy a regular wage, though whether that could be described as a 'living wage' is debatable. The Church remains dependent on financial help from mission agencies, overseas friends, and partners, mainly in the United States, especially where new initiatives or projects are concerned. This financial dependence, which many parts of the Anglican Communion experience, may also distort the current theological debates taking place.

When we are faced with requests from partners in Ghana for financial assistance, as the forty or so parishes with active links in the Diocese of Portsmouth often are, the question arises of whether the assistance we give will help or hinder in making the Anglican Church in Ghana more self-sufficient and less economically dependent. It is the same question NGOs and charities are asking of the projects they support. There are some visionary projects in dioceses and parishes and villages which aim precisely at generating regular income. Both the Dioceses of Sunyani and Cape Coast have set up a water filtering process so that they can retail clean water to earn income. The Dioceses of Accra and Kumasi both have farms producing fruit and vege-tables. The Diocese of Koforidua is planning to set up a palm oil plantation. Some parishes can see a future in set-ting up a small farm or renting land for shops or stalls. The small village of Buriton in Hampshire has helped its linked village of Dominase in Central Region with the provision of water from wells. This will benefit both health and the local economy. The bridge across the river and the solar power generator in the remote village of Ayiesu in Eastern Region, supported by funds from churches on Hayling Island in

Hampshire are similar examples. It is particularly necessary to support these sorts of projects for local income generation and other kinds of endowment. From self-sufficiency comes self-motivation.

The Diocese of Kumasi is currently planning to set up a Retreat and Conference Centre, as a place of Christian learning and training, and has asked its friends in Portsmouth for help and advice. This poses a dilemma, less about finance and more about the relationship between culture and prayer. Help and advice will be offered, though questions will naturally arise about how much the Western spiritual tradition will assist in complementing and developing African forms of spirituality. What will they make of Mother Julian or Celtic prayer in rural Ashanti? On the other hand, the wisdom of Benedict, and the balance in his teaching between work and prayer, may be particularly suited to the context of Ghana.

The legacy which the Church of England has left to the Anglican Church in Ghana includes a cultural and economic dependence. If we have an uneasy conscience about the role our Christian forbears played in the slave trade, one positive step forward will be to walk alongside our Christian friends in Ghana as they try to move on from the cultural and economic dependence which we have bequeathed them. That is the most effective apology for slavery that we can make.

For both Churches, the context of the task of mission is strikingly similar – a minority church with an establishment background seeking to communicate the good news of Jesus Christ in ways that local culture can recognise, access, and embrace. Recognising this as an inherited and shared common task will help to put in perspective the current strains and tensions within the Anglican Communion.

Notes

1 Letter to the Committee of Merchants (1837) in George Edgar
   Metcalfe, *Great Britain and Ghana: Documents of Ghana History
   1807–1957* (London, 1964).
2 Quoted in William St Clair, *The Grand Slave Emporium* (London: Profile Books, 2006).
3 Quoted in St Clair, op. cit.
4 Quoted in St Clair, op. cit.
5 Quoted in St Clair, op. cit.
6 J. S. Pobee, *Invitation to be an African Anglican* (Accra: Asempa
   Publishers, 2000).
7 Quoted in Pobee, op. cit.
8 Pobee, op. cit.

3

David Stancliffe

The Episcopal Church in the Sudan and its Emerging Ecclesiology

The relationship between the Province of the Episcopal Church of the Sudan and the Diocese of Salisbury has become a vital aspect of church life from its inception. The partnership – in which the relationship between the bishops and in particular between the Archbishops and the Bishops of Salisbury has been significant – has been and remains unbroken over the years. I want to illustrate this developing relationship by what might be called a series of Green Guide-style snapshots, each of which introduces a particular ecclesiological slant.

Our link with the Province of the Sudan has been running for some thirty-five years, and is a major factor in the life of the diocese. Even when the civil war between the north and south was at its height, our visits and exchanges continued, and we are regarded, with CMS, as their oldest and most significant partners. Our bishops and theirs meet frequently to exchange ideas and support one another. As a result, much of the theological education of the clergy is supported by us, as are the modest medical centres in many of the dioceses in the south. Now that peace has come, with the prospect of a degree of independence for the south, there is an urgent task to build up together the resources, in terms of teachers and buildings, that will support secondary education where practically none exists, as the foundation for the future.

In parallel, there is rarely a moment when one bishop or another from the Province of the Sudan is not visiting us, and several have undertaken major study here. In the summer, we have regularly had exchanges, and in particular their young youth leaders have brought a vision of life and vitality to our young people and parishes. Their bishops and the Archbishop in particular provide valuable sources of information to our Foreign and International Development Offices and Parliamentary Committees, and are always made welcome in Whitehall. We share this partnership with the Diocese of Bradford in the north of England. They have a twinning with the Diocese of Khartoum, and extend their support to the other three dioceses in the northern part of Sudan as well. But our link with the Province as a whole continues to be a reality.

The Consecration of the New Cathedral at Renk

As our helicopter came lumbering out of the skies, we could see the circle where we were to land marked out in a vast dusty square. We stepped out into the chanting crowds, and were hoisted into the back of an open truck. Huge numbers of Sudanese – virtually the entire community of the diocese – started running to keep up with us. The air was filled with swirling dust, and as I clung precariously to the braided epaulettes of the Chief of Police, I felt like an extra in some desert film like *Lawrence of Arabia*.

But it wasn't Arabia: it was Renk, a town that lies on the border between northern and southern Sudan, and I was there to participate in the consecration of its new cathedral by the Archbishop of Canterbury – an event of enormous significance for the church in Sudan.

The very existence of the church in Renk, let alone the feat of building a cathedral there, shines a ray of hope into an otherwise bleak landscape. But built it they have. The dome over the east end is lit at night by swirls of multi-coloured bulbs which make Blackpool look sober by comparison. It is easily the tallest building in this town, which lies on the borderlands of Arab north and the Christian south of the country, and the local Imam was delighted to have been invited to the consecration. The procession, accompanied by singing and dancing, winds round the outside of the cathedral sprinkling it with water, and again, stopping at the four corners, to anoint them with oil. Inside, all is shiny and new, and donors from the diocese in the Episcopal Church in the USA who took a major part in funding Bishop Daniel's cathedral contrast vividly with the dark noses of the small boys who press their faces to the windows. Some hours in to the liturgy, Archbishop Joseph finishes a prayer, and steps forward to address the congregation. With an ear-splitting crash, the immense chandelier comes adrift from its moorings and smashes into smithereens on the floor, just where the Archbishop had been standing a moment before. Without a flicker, the Archbishop continues, and the remains are hastily swept away. God has preserved the Archbishop, and a church that has endured the physical dangers of years of civil war is not going to be put off its stride by a tinkling glass or a clashing chandelier.

As we leave from the little airstrip in Renk next morning,

I observe the carcasses of many cattle, victims of drought and disaster. Their bones stick out of the remnants of skin and their skulls gleam white in the dust. Seeing them, I think of the prophet Ezekiel's vision of the valley of dry bones (Ezekiel 37:1–14), with its promise that out of the dry desert God will bring new life and make of his scattered people a united, living force.

If we need a sign of the power of God at work in our world, we need look no further than Renk. In spite of the many years of civil war, with virtually none of the resources we would consider essential for sustaining even basic life, these people have stood on their feet – a vast multitude. They are a remarkable witness to the power of God to fill the dry bones of his Church with the breath of his living spirit. This is the foundation of our relationship: the power of God to make all thinks new, to be leading us from our present into his future. Everything in the Sudan has this eschatological reference: 'when peace comes', 'when we have the promised schools', 'when the people come back to rebuild our life'.

The Recent History of the Episcopal Church of the Sudan

I begin with this vignette to illustrate the context in which the Episcopal Church of the Sudan, to give it its proper title, has matured and blossomed since the country received independence more than half a century ago. The country was historically part of the CMS mission territory, and Sudanese Christians, though distantly aware of a Nubian Coptic past which lasted from the mid-sixth century until its collapse and Islamisation by around 1500, date their conversion to Christianity from the closing months of the nineteenth century, and hail among their founding fathers missionary evangelicals like Archdeacon Archibald Shaw. By the time Bishop Oliver Allison resigned in the 1960s and the first African was appointed, Sudan, a country roughly four times the size of France, was a separate diocese from Egypt, with whom it had been joined in colonial days. By the early 1970s, the number of bishops had increased to four; by the turn of the twenty-first century, there were twenty-four; there is now a commission reporting on how to manage the continuing expansion of the church: will there be half a dozen more dioceses in a year's time?

This extraordinary growth has taken place almost entirely within a context of a bitter civil war between the north and the south of the country. Apart from a brief period in the 1980s, fighting continued for some forty years, exhausting both sides in a conflict that has essentially been between the north, which has cultural affinities with an Arab upper Egypt, and the south, which is part of central Africa. The north is substantially Islamic, and has only four of the twenty-four dioceses of the Province, while the south, African and animist by cultural background, is now very substantially Christian and has the other twenty dioceses. In its final phase, the war has been fought over the substantial oil reserves, which lie near the border between north and south, but which the north has been desperate to control. The fragile Comprehensive Peace Agreement, brokered by the charismatic leader of the Sudan Peoples Liberation Army, Dr John Garang, was nearly derailed by his death in a helicopter accident in July 2005 not long after it had started to become effective, and his tomb in Juba, the ancient capital of the south, has the trappings of a martyr's shrine.

One of the factors responsible for the rapid growth of the

Christian faith in the south was the failure – as it was perceived – of the old animist gods to preserve the Dinka
people and their cattle. A great bonfire of the *jok*, the traditional idols, accompanied a wholesale conversion to the
new faith, and Isaiah's language of rescue and redemption
coupled with an Old Testament theology of the land
seemed to fit their context exactly. This has left the church
of the Province with a baptismal rather than eucharistic
theology at the heart of its life, a sense of being drawn from
darkness into light, of always standing on the threshold and
of being at a point of challenge, rather than a more settled
abiding in Christ and growing in mature Christian discipleship. A church fashioned under crisis lays its emphasis
on making new disciples, on bringing people to the point of
decision, rather than on nurturing and deepening the faith
of those who are already members of the body. While the
role of bishops in leading the church in mission, in
ordaining new pastors, and in baptising and confirming is
widely understood, there has been less emphasis on the
continuing formation of the ordained and in celebrating the
Eucharist. Sermons are often based on Old Testament
texts, and the native tradition of Sudanese hymnody often
uses imagery from the Exodus and Exile.

This is an ecclesiology which is born out of the extraordinary context in which the church has been formed, and
is significantly different from either the inherited, cumulative ecclesiology of the Church of England, which is largely
implicit, or that of much of the rest of the Anglican Communion, where the church has evolved gradually out of the
colonial 'plant'. There is another factor which is parallel to
the distinctive relationship that the Sudan has enjoyed with
the United Kingdom. In the first half of the twentieth
century, Sudan did not fall under the Colonial Service. The

condominium had its own Sudan Civil Service, and to this day former members whose affection for the Sudanese has never wavered are still loyally supporting the Sudan Church Association. This sense of a special relationship has meant that the Episcopal Church of the Sudan has enjoyed a close relationship with the Archbishop of Canterbury.

An Archiepiscopal Election

In 2000, I attended the General Synod of the Episcopal Church of the Sudan. I had been invited by Joseph Marona, then Bishop of Maridi and Dean of the Province, to attend their meeting and lead a retreat with them in preparation.

This was no ordinary meeting of a synod. Under their constitution, drafted when the Province became independent in 1976, the bishop with two clergy and two lay people from each diocese form the electoral college to choose a new archbishop. That seemed a reasonable number in 1976 when the infant Province had four dioceses, but now, with the huge increase in numbers of Christians, there are twenty-four. Part of the reason for this enormous growth is the longing for a just and free society, which is what fuelled the civil war that had divided the country in two for forty-five years, with an Islamic government in the north and much of the more African south under the control of the Sudan Peoples Liberation Army. But the war meant that there was nowhere the whole church could meet together in the Sudan, so upwards of one hundred and twenty people had to be transported to Limuru in Kenya.

This was achieved at enormous cost to the Sudanese Church's partners and well-wishers, but proved to be worth every penny. Fellow-Christians who had not met for twenty years prayed, lived, and talked together. Suspicions fostered by hearsay began to melt, and the lay people especially seemed determined to step beyond the north/south divide. The genuine desire for reconciliation that even a short experience of common life fostered began to dispel even the deeply ingrained tribal antagonism, and a tribal caucus, summoned to try and deliver a block vote for a particular candidate, was not persuaded to behave tribally, even though there were persistent rumours of large bribes being offered. Instead, the commitment to several days' study, prayer, and reflection as the basis for what was to be undertaken was remarkable. I caught myself wondering if the business was ever going to get underway as the after-echoes rumbled on and on, but then reflected that if the General Synod of the Church of England spent as much time in prayer as theirs, we in England might find it easier to come – as they did – to a common mind which everyone accepted.

When we eventually got to the election and the register of electors had been publicly checked and the procedural questions sorted – we spent quite a time discussing how a pair of assessors (there were four judges among the House of Laity) would need to go into the voting booth with an elector who could not write, only to discover that there were none! – the Provincial Chancellor called for nominations. Two came at once, then another, and finally a fourth, and the list was closed. They called for prayer, kept an intense silence, and then the voting began. Each elector was called forward in turn, verified, given a slip with the Chancellor's signature on it and led to a booth at the back of the stage before returning to place their ballot paper in the box in the sight of all. Voting began shortly after 10pm, and took an hour and a half. Then interest quickened. The assessors tipped out the box, and showed it empty to the assembly.

The slips were then counted to make sure that there were the right number; great sighs of relief as the right total was reached. Only then did the three judges start reading out the names, and all three scrutinised each paper in turn, after which the vote was chalked up against the candidate on the faint blackboard.

Quite early on it became clear that the majority of the votes were going to Joseph Marona, the Dean, and the excitement mounted. And so it turned out to be. When the last vote was counted, and midnight had struck, it was clear that he had over twenty more votes than all the other candidates put together. But although the constitution spoke at a later stage of an 'absolute majority', all it actually said about the first stage was that the candidate with the fewest votes – one had only five – dropped off the list, and unless the leading candidate had two-thirds of the votes the process had to be re-run. It looked as if we were in for a long night.

But then, with the graciousness that comes only with a commitment to seek God's will, the candidate who had the next smallest number – nineteen – withdrew, and the Chancellor waited to see what the candidate with twenty-five would do. He was clearly torn, as he had wanted the office in the way that Joseph Marona clearly had not. After only a moment's hesitation, he also withdrew. Joseph was duly declared elected. In the event, he was – clearly – reluctant, and left the assembly to spend the remainder of this night in prayer, to test his heart to see if he could say yes.

The graciousness and dignity of the elected and electors alike in this prayerful process was remarkable. In the end the choice fell on the most transparent of the candidates: when morning came he said yes, and declared at once that their collective task was to reconcile a torn church in a divided country, and that this could only be done by making the way they worked together visible in every moment. This was indeed going to be a hard task, in the face of the forces of tribalism, the inherited culture of nepotism, and a history of getting what power you can for yourself and your dependants in a country of deep division and desperate poverty that threaten to undermine every stage of the process. But the signal the church gave to the political leaders of both north and south Sudan has been loud and clear: sacrificial love and deep prayer can overcome the forces of darkness and bring reconciliation. This is not our achievement; it is God's. In the motto of Canon Ezra, who was killed in the civil war (and which forms the title of the centenary history of the Episcopal Church in the Sudan), 'God is not defeated'.

The Ordination of Women

After that, the other business of the General Synod in 2000 seemed tame. There were other important elections to the office of Provincial Secretary and Treasurer. There were questions of how to draft and test amendments to the constitution, and how to set up a Provincial Tribunal to handle the irregularities in a Province that has grown like Topsy.

Most significant though was the debate on the ordination of women, when by an overwhelming majority, they passed the motion that 'The General Synod of the E.C.S. believing that there is no theological reason why women should not be ordained, agrees in principle to the ordination of women to the diaconate, the priesthood and the episcopate; and gives discretion to each Diocesan Bishop, with the agreement of the Diocesan Synod, as to when to introduce the practice.' In the debate, much time was given to reporting the views of the different dioceses, but there was less concern for the theological arguments. Nothing in Scripture or the tradition actually forbade the possibility; and did not the apostle say that in Christ there was to be neither Jew nor Greek, male or female, bond or free? Did a ministry of only one gender reflect the inclusive ministry of Christ, or were not both male and female necessary to offer a visible icon of the inclusive ministry he offered? Rather there was a great desire for the church to make a positive statement about the inherent equality of men and women before God in a culture where traditionally this has not been so. In some dioceses where a high proportion of the men and boys are away fighting, it was the women who were leading the church, as they were holding together the local community. This too was seen as an important statement of the church's Gospel of the new creation.

It was remarkable to witness this process, and to see how mission imperatives outweighed other considerations. There was the baptismal imperative of the absolute equality of men and women within the body of Christ. There was the challenge of Islam: the Muslims 'treat their women abominably, and we should do better', we were told. Perhaps surprisingly however, in a traditionally conservative and biblically serious church, there was no appeal to the doctrine of male headship: the equality and complementarity of the sexes, within a theology of creation where 'male and female he created them' in the image and likeness of God was perceived to override the Pauline instructions to particular churches in difficulty in ordering their lives, is felt to be an overriding truth. In a church where at least half the congregations were female, did we not need women priests to minister among them? Could an all-male priesthood ever model that inclusive love of God made visible in Christ?

The Medical Link

One of the important areas where salvation can be given hard currency is health. In many of the southern dioceses there are now small clinics and pharmacies in the bishop's compound where basic testing for a number of the commonest diseases – malaria, tuberculosis, and yellow fever – can be carried out, the relevant drugs administered, and the basics of clean water and health education taught. But now that there is sufficient peace to enable the basic infrastructure of roads and bridges to be rebuilt and the channels of communication begin to open up again, there are hazards as well as blessings ahead. It may indeed mean that there is more chance of exporting the wonderful fruit and vegetables from the fertile south, but roads and bridges mean trucks and truckers, and in a country where AIDS has a comparatively low incidence, that scourge will spread like wildfire with the truckers unless there is a major programme of health education.

Partnership with the Roman Catholic Bishops' Conference

Another element in the life of the Province which has been growing is the quality of the relationship between the bishops of the ECS and their Roman Catholic counterparts. In a context like that of the war-torn Sudan, there was so much more that the churches had in common. Both preach the same Gospel; both use the identical Scriptures; both celebrate the sacraments of the new covenant; both belong within a world-wide communion that preserves them from a narrow parochialism; both have the same things to say about the pursuit of peace and justice.

At a colloquium in Rome, drawing together members of both ecclesial communions, a pattern of support was worked out which has enabled the bishops of both churches in the Sudan to meet together to study, pray, and build up a common life. Neither would speak out in public on social and political issues without a common mind and a single statement. To hear Archbishop Paulino and Archbishop Joseph speaking together in a public forum, you never knew who would speak whose lines, because they seemed so interchangeable; and in a town like Malakal, where the bishops are among a very small number of educated leaders, their companionship is clearly personally important as well as ecumenically significant.

Another area in which the co-operation between the churches is important for the future is in education, and in particular the vitally important area of secondary education. There are very few secondary schools in southern Sudan, and such as there are are mostly ill-equipped, and thinly staffed from neighbouring countries. If there are no adequate secondary schools for their children, it will be difficult to persuade those able Sudanese who have found an education in other countries to return and help develop a future for their country. There is great potential for working together across denominational boundaries to deliver the tools for a future: joint investment in the training of teachers, especially at secondary level, is the most pressing need of the country, and the churches are the only agency with the resources on the ground to enable this to happen.

Personal Links and the Basis of Trust

Archbishop Joseph was a secondary school headteacher before he was ordained. Travelling through remote villages with him after he became Archbishop and waving to those at the roadside, I noticed a broad smile of recognition would often pass over his face as he'd point and say, 'That's Abraham: I used to teach him.' So we'd stop the car and greet Abraham and his neighbours, delighted that after all these years he had been recognised, and was known by name.

Fear not, for I have redeemed you; I have called you by name, you are mine. When you pass through the waters, I will be with you; and through the rivers, they shall not overwhelm you; when you walk through the fire you shall not be burned, and the flame shall not consume you. For I am the Lord your God, the Holy One of Israel, your Saviour. (Isaiah 43:1b–3a)

Even in a country as vast as Sudan, it is being recognised and known by name that counts in building the relationship between the very local and the entirely unknown world which is believed to be so unimaginably vital to their hope of a future beyond. I was astonished to find when I first went to the Sudan how important this was, and that my visit was seen as a sign that the poor and dispossessed in distant parts of southern Sudan were not forgotten. Even now that peace has come, these visits are recalled: 'Bishop David is our friend: even when it was difficult and dangerous he came to be with us.' I did not do anything or say anything, except to assure them of our prayers and that they were not forgotten; but this was enough to forge the links of friendship and trust, without which so little can be achieved.

I suppose that the basis of our relationship, and why there is no question in any of our minds as to whether the bonds of communion could be threatened by the questions which seem to have become the defining issue in other parts of the Anglican Communion, is secured on our standing together over the really important matters of life and death, peace and freedom, and the power of the Gospel to change lives. When, in the five-yearly meeting of their General Synod in Juba in January 2005, we came to the agenda item on Human Sexuality, there was a brief discussion. There was little appetite for debate, as it is generally recognised in the Sudan that while definitions of terms used in Sudan in the debate about human sexuality are coloured by memories of a late-nineteenth-century Buganda of Uganda's perverted sexual preferences, we are united in resisting the exploitation of people of either sex at any stage by anyone. After about ten minutes, the bishop chairing the discussion proposed that we move to next business, on the grounds that there were many more important issues confronting the church in the Sudan that were central to the proclamation of the Gospel and the mission of the church. This proposal was warmly received, and the Synod moved on.

What underlies this reluctance to spend time on what would be regarded as secondary issues is partly the urgency of the missionary situation in the Sudan. In the dialogue with Islam it is tempting to regard the Bible as somehow the equivalent of the Koran, an absolute guide to the complete and final revelation of the Holy One. Christians know that the books of the Bible cannot be treated in this way, as a monolithic statement of the final and absolute Word of God: that description can only be applied to the living word of God, Jesus Christ himself. The Christian insight, celebrated in our worship, is that the God whom we worship is engaged with us; that the faith is relational rather than propositional; that the discovery that God is a Trinity of persons places us into a dynamic rather than a static relationship with him, and that change – personal, ecclesial, and social – is the central expectation of the followers of Christ. 'Metanoiéte', usually rendered in the older translations of the gospels as 'repent', means 'change your mind', or – as a teenager of today might say – 'get a life'.

Our partners in the Sudan regularly challenge us with the demands of the Gospel to change, and get a life. When we read the gospels together, we are challenged to explore what it is that brings us life. Where are the signs of the new creation taking root? Where is the kingdom breaking through? What is it that the church has to offer the exhausted and despairing people of the Sudan, north and south, as they struggle to get a life? These are the questions at the heart of our common endeavour, and what has emerged is not a paternalistic system of fawning dependency or a tough-minded sense of independence: it is rather a proper pattern of interdependence within the body of Christ, which is – at the end of the day – what we are really called to embody within the Communion as a mark of our maturity.

4

James Jones

Making Space for Truth and Grace: Akure, Virginia, and Liverpool

The Anglican Communion as it is: a new initiative

However else you may wish to define and describe the Anglican Communion the reality is that it consists of myriad relationships between dioceses, deaneries, parishes, and Provinces around the globe. Like a map from an in-flight magazine that shows the airline's routes criss-crossing the world, so the Anglican Church offers a network of links that connect people from different cultures. It lacks the structured pattern of a spider's web because these connecting strands do not emerge from the strategic planning department of a central secretariat. Rather it resembles a spilled bowl of spaghetti! This image is not to belittle the Communion but to recognise that the shapelessness of the Communion is part of its history and its character.

Although there have been attempts to order and to organise the Communion the reality is that dioceses, deaneries, and parishes have over the years exercised great freedom in entering into relationships with one another.

And again, although guidelines exist to steer these partnerships the fact is they are shaped much more by need,
experience, enthusiasm, and friendship. It means that
whatever formal relationships exist between Primates and
Provinces there exists at another level an untidy yet surprisingly strong set of mature relationships that have stood
the test of time. The Diocese of Liverpool is in formal
partnerships with two other Dioceses – Akure and Virginia.

The driving force behind me initiating a tripartite conversation on sexuality was the idea that the debate about
contentious subjects is best located in these already established relationships. It is better to deal with difficult ethical
and doctrinal questions – in this case, sexuality – in a
conversation between people who already know, trust, and
respect each other than through megaphone diplomacy
between strangers across the oceans. The historic partnerships within the Anglican Communion can offer a different
context for the debate about homosexuality where there can
be a genuine dialogue between people whose mutual trust
and affection protect them from jumping too soon to conclusions and keep them in conversation because a long time
ago they learned to think the best and not the worst of each
other.

One of the things that happens when conversations
begin, especially when they involve more than two people,
is that you begin to see that there are more than two sides to
an argument. In a media-dominated world everything is
polarised in a most reductionist way and even the most
complex issues are reduced to whether you are for or
against a particular subject. This treatment does not do
justice to the complexity of ethical discourse and ill serves
the people most affected by the debate. One of the dis-
coveries I found in our conversation about homosexuality

between the continents of Africa, Europe, and America is that there was a variety of insights, perspectives, and opinions that defied the way the media polarise the debate into simply two clear-cut oppositional positions and want always to reduce complex and nuanced positions into the half-truths of soundbites. This is not to deny that in the end an ethical decision has to be taken. What it recognises is that there needs to be more space along the way for people to view the terrain from different vantage points. But it is difficult to maintain this space, especially under pressure from the world-wide media whose tendency is to dramatise, to polarise, and to present every issue in terms of extreme opposites. This is not the place for an essay on the media, and there is much that is good about a communications industry that has raised international public awareness of global poverty and the environment. But one of the tensions that Christians struggle with in the modern world is that we live and move and have our being in a globe saturated by media that drive people apart through this polarising tendency and produce a dynamic in human relationships at odds with the reconciling and unifying movement of the Gospel.

Some will point to our history and to the Scriptures for the need to act decisively and will interpret this plea for space as a lack of courage and leadership. What I have found in our tripartite conversation is that the space has yielded new insights, not least because that space has been protected by an established relationship in Christ of trust and affection.

In Acts 15 the Council of Jerusalem was dogged by controversy. What was at stake was the essence of the Gospel. There was dissension and debate about the means of salvation. This was a first-order issue. Some Christians

were insisting that salvation required the Gentile converts
to be circumcised. 'Unless you are circumcised according to
the custom of Moses, you cannot be saved' (15:1). What I
find of special significance for how Christians handle controversy is that Luke describes these detractors as 'believers'. Even though the doctrine they were proposing
undermined the doctrine of grace and of justification
through faith the author included them within the body of
believers. Within that space there was heated debate as they
wrestled for the truth. This example has informed my own
attitude and practice when it comes to theological and
ethical debates, offering and in turn hoping for a generosity
of spirit and the space to question and to listen to different
interpretations and experiences of both first- and second-
order issues.

It also makes me quizzical about the talk of 'impaired
communion' which itself seems to undermine the doctrine
of grace and certainly shrinks the space within which to
have frank theological debate.

We are in Christ by the grace of God. None of us earns or
merits that place. In Christ we find ourselves alongside and
at one (whether we like it – or them – or not) with all others
who by God's grace are also in Christ. We cannot take
ourselves into Christ, neither can we remove another from
being in Christ. It is all by grace. Now it is clear that controversy can impair friendship, can affect ministry, and even
undermine mission but only Christ can determine communion, with him and through him with one another. As in
the Council of Jerusalem and the controversy over doctrine
and practice so today in the Anglican Communion there
may be impaired mission, impaired ministry, impaired
friendship but as to 'communion' that is only and forever in
and through Christ alone.

The Conversations in Process

These are the sentiments that have informed the debate about human sexuality in the Diocese of Liverpool and encouraged us to take the initiative to discuss it with our partner dioceses.

Within the diocese of Liverpool I have called for the debate to be set within a new framework, within a forum of four walls, recognising that each of the four sides is a vital part of the forum of discussion:

The first point of the quadrilateral is to recognise the authoritative biblical emphasis upon the uniqueness of marriage as a divine ordinance for the ordering of human society and the nurture of children.

The second is to acknowledge the authoritative biblical examples of love between two people of the same gender most notably in the relationship of Jesus and his beloved and David and Jonathan.

The third is to register the role of conscience in the Anglican moral tradition; in the Church of England's oaths of canonical obedience the vow is to be obedient 'in all things lawful and honest' which means that should you be pressed to do something which in good conscience you deem not to be honest then conscience would demand that you dissent.

The fourth point is to understand that disunity saps the energy of the church and to affirm the importance of unity to the mission of God.

Each of these sides merits closer inspection and deserves its own essay. But the point I want to make is that holding these four together has produced space within the diocese for us to have a genuine conversation.

The 1998 Lambeth Conference asked us to be in dialogue with people and as a result of that in 2001 I invited Professor Ian Markham, then Professor of Public Theology at Liverpool Hope University and now Dean of Virginia Theological Seminary, to chair a group exploring 'A Theology of Friendship'. The group's membership reflected the diversity of opinion, theological, ethical, and ecclesiastical and was inclusive of gender. The group worked for two years with occasional residential consultations and needed all that time to build trust so that honest discussion could take place. Although I was not part of the group my own thinking has been informed by their findings. In particular I have continued to reflect on the biblical material. The quality of the group's work has set the tone for the debate in the diocese which is an important contribution to our common life and to the mission of God, for energy is not being sapped by internal strife.

The 'Theology of Friendship' Report took me in particular to the relationship between David and Jonathan. Their friendship was emotional, spiritual, and even physical. Jonathan loved David 'as his own soul'. David found Jonathan's love for him, 'passing the love of women'. There was between them a deep emotional bond that left David grief-stricken when Jonathan died. But not only were they emotionally bound to each other they expressed their love physically. Jonathan stripped off his clothes and dressed David in his own robe and armour. With the candour of the Eastern world that exposes the reserve of Western culture they kissed each other and wept openly with each other. The fact that they were both married did not inhibit them in emotional and physical displays of love for each other. This intimate relationship was sealed before God. It was not just a spiritual bond, it became covenantal for 'Jonathan made a covenant with David, because he loved him as his own soul' (1 Samuel 18:3). Here is the Bible bearing witness to love between two people of the same gender. I know that at this point some will ask, 'Was the friendship sexual?', 'Were they gay?', 'Was at least one of them homosexual?', 'Were they both heterosexual?', 'Were they bisexual?' I want to resist these questions at least initially. Immediately you start using such words you conjure up stereotypes and prejudices. Further, you assume that it is a person's sexual inclination that defines their personhood. Is it not possible to say that here are two men with the capacity to love fully, both women and men?

The intimacy between David and Jonathan is also evident in the relationship between the Son of David and his beloved John. We find the two at one with each other during the supper when Jesus washes the feet of his disciples. The beloved disciple is found reclining next to Jesus. Translations are not adequate to the text. Two different phrases are used in John 13, verses 23 and 25. One of them says literally that John was leaning against the bosom, breast, chest of Jesus (*kolpos*).

No English word or phrase fully captures the closeness of the liaison. What is significant is that the word used in John 13:23 is found only on one other occasion in the Gospel of John. In John 1:18 the word is used to describe the intimate relationship between 'God the only Son' and the Father. 'No one has ever seen God. It is God the only Son who is close to the Father's heart (*kolpos*) who has made him known.' It is difficult for a human being to conceive of a closer relationship than that between the Persons of the Holy Trinity. That this word is used of the relationship between Jesus and John is a remarkable expression of the love between the two men. This love finds expression on several occasions. On the cross Jesus makes his beloved friend his mother's son in an extraordinary covenant of love and on the day of the Resurrection love propels the bereaved and beloved disciple to outrun Peter and arrive first at the tomb. Here is energising love, spiritual, emotional, and physical.

It is with reflections such as these that I entered with anticipation into the dialogue with our partner dioceses within the Anglican Communion. I also came, as we all do to every encounter, with a history. I had been one of the nine diocesan bishops to have objected publicly to the proposed consecration of Dr Jeffrey John, now Dean of St Albans. I deeply regret this episode in our common life. I regret too having objected publicly without first having consulted with the Archbishops of York and Canterbury, and subsequently apologised to them and to colleagues in a private meeting of the House of Bishops. I still believe that it was unwise to try to take us to a place that evidently did not command the broad support of the Church of England but I am sorry for the way I opposed it and I am sorry too for adding to the pain and distress of Dr John and his partner. I regret too that this particular controversy narrowed rather than enlarged the space for healthy debate within the church.

I have wrestled with writing the above for fear of opening old wounds but I cannot give a true account of my part in the continuing debate without acknowledging the history I brought to the table. In the same way (and they must speak for themselves) the bishops and correspondents from Africa and America needed to acknowledge their own stories in coming to the conversation.

We have had two residential conferences within the tri-partite conversation. In April 2005 Liverpool invited Akure and in November 2006 invited both Akure and Virginia. Agreed statements describe the process and the substance of our reflections, to which I am not at liberty to add. In each case the conversation was facilitated by Stephen Lyon whose skills added indisputably to the quality of the conversation.

These encounters in England, together with my own visits to America and Africa, have enabled me to study the Scriptures with greater cultural awareness. I have a deeper and more affectionate understanding of both Africa and America. I can see how the Church of Nigeria's response to the sexuality debate is contextualised. The law of their land prohibits homosexual acts. It is therefore difficult for the church to be party to an international debate about a practice that is actually outlawed and illegal. Whatever moral view one takes and however much one denounces the persecution and oppression that has ensued it is possible to acknowledge the challenge of their cultural context. Fur-thermore, in Africa as elsewhere in the world there is a battle with Islam for the hearts and minds of the masses of the population. African Christianity wants to guard itself from the charge that it is a front for Western imperialism in decadent decline. Associating with the agenda and sexual mores of American and European societies allows Chris-tianity's Islamic critics to portray the church in Africa as compromised, weak, and in moral decline. These are ser-ious missiological issues which need to be recognised and understood, rather than pilloried and dismissed.

The same is true for America, where the proposers of change are also subject to caricature. The Civil Rights movement has a much greater grip on the soul of America than it does on either England or Europe generally. For many in the Episcopal Church the rights of gay and lesbian people are seen as unequivocally akin to the rights of African-Americans. There is a poignant irony here for it is with Africans from contemporary Africa that many American Episcopalians are most at odds in a cause that they feel parallels the plight of and the fight for justice by their ancestors who came to America two centuries earlier. Gay rights are civil rights. It is a matter of natural justice. Failure to understand this at best mystifies and at worst angers the majority in the Episcopal Church that was once so guiltily complicit in slavery and is now so anxious to shake off the shackles of the past and prove its commitment to social justice which is such an important strand in the prophetic literature of the Bible. These are serious historical and contemporary moral and social perspectives that need to be understood in the international debate about human sexuality.

What I have learned from our ongoing tripartite conversation is that we need to have and protect the space for genuine dialogue in the spirit of Lambeth 1.10. I worry about the Windsor proposals not because I doubt the courage and integrity of those who are working on them but because I fear that they will take us in the direction of narrowing the space and of closing down the debate on this and any future issue where Christians find themselves in conversation with their culture on some new moral development or dilemma. The result is that energy is sapped by internal definitions rather than released into engaging with the world so loved of God.

The description in John's Gospel of Jesus 'full of grace and truth' presents us with a person who created space around himself for others to 'see the Kingdom of God'. He was neither truthless in his grace, nor graceless in his truth. I fear that in our debates with each other and with the world, especially on the subject of homosexuality, we have come over as graceless. Jesus was a pastor, as well as a prophet. He spoke commandments with compassion. And when in John 8 he was asked to judge an adulterer he said 'Neither do I condemn you' before adding 'Go away and sin no more'. The Pastor spoke before the Prophet. Had it been the other way around she would not have been there to hear his words of mercy. I am not here equating homosexuality with adultery but simply registering the priority Jesus gave to the pastoral approach.

I know there are some – from all sides of the argument – who might feel that to be in conversation with those with whom you profoundly disagree is to legitimise their own position and compromise your own. I know too that the continuing debate does not alleviate the suffering of those most affected. In this time we are particularly dependent on the grace of those who are hurt by the words and actions of others. All I know and can testify to through our own discussions within the diocese and with our partner dioceses is that entering the debate prayerfully in the company of the One who is 'full of grace and truth' takes you to places beyond 'all that you can ask or imagine'. I know that many are pessimistic about the future but I find myself strangely and surprisingly optimistic that if we can maintain the space to listen to 'the still small voice' there might emerge a new understanding and paradigm that none of us can yet imagine.

This is a personal essay and has not been written on behalf of the other two Dioceses.

PART TWO

Unfinished Business

5

Graham James

Resolving to Confer and Conferring to Resolve: the Anglican way

The First Lambeth Conference

Bishops stayed away in considerable numbers from the first Lambeth Conference. In February 1867 the Archbishop of Canterbury, Charles Longley, issued an invitation to the whole Anglican episcopate to attend. Seventy-six bishops did so. One hundred and fifty-one were invited. Some were prevented by distance or infirmity or both. Australia and India were represented by a single bishop each. But quite a number stayed away on principle. The Archbishop of York refused to attend, as did every other bishop in his Province, except Chester. The Bishop of Peterborough likewise refused. The venerable Bishop of St David's, Connop Thirlwall, was minded to decline since he thought the conference would inevitably seek to modify the constitution and government of the Church of England. He was fearful that bishops from the United States and the colonies would outvote those at home. The Bishop of London, Archibald Campbell Tait, was equally anxious about the authority of such a gathering. He sought an assurance from the Archbishop that the limits of the competence of the conference should be specified carefully beforehand. Hence Archbishop Longley stated in his letter of invitation that 'such a meeting as is proposed would not be competent to make declarations or lay down definitions on points of doctrine'.

So the Lambeth Conference was not to be a Synod or a Council. It was an invitation to confer. Nothing more. As things have turned out, Lambeth Conferences have not been bashful about declaring to the world the collective mind of the Anglican episcopate. Perhaps it was Longley's promise that caused them to opt for resolutions rather than declarations or definitions, along with a substantial number of pastoral letters and lengthy reports. The difficulty with resolutions, however, is that they don't always resolve the problems they address. That's partly because those who are intimately connected with the problems or even the cause of them are not always present. Even so, sometimes the Lambeth bishops have had a decisive impact upon the mind of the Anglican Communion as a whole.

A major shift in thinking on birth control between the 1920 and 1930 Conferences saved the Anglican Communion from the convulsions experienced by the Roman Catholic Church in the 1960s and which still affect its life. The Lambeth bishops were cautiously brave in 1930. They recognised that there were morally sound reasons both to limit or avoid parenthood in marriage and for married couples to avoid complete sexual abstinence. This was scarcely uncontroversial. The resolution favouring contraception passed by 193 votes to 67. It was a decisive vote but not unanimous. The Lambeth bishops in 1930 went on to condemn the use of any method of conception control from motives of selfishness, luxury, or mere convenience. They thought that contraception should not be used as a way of meeting unsatisfactory social and economic conditions. They also pressed (largely unsuccessfully) for legislation which would forbid the unrestricted advertisement of contraceptives and wanted definite restrictions upon their purchase. 'Cautiously brave' seems the best way to describe the change but it was fundamental nonetheless.

Some of the bishops in the minority felt a betrayal of Christian teaching and doctrine had taken place. Walter Carey, the Bishop of Bloemfontein, withdrew from the Conference in protest, refused to attend the closing service and even sent a petition on the matter to the King. The Bishop of Exeter equated contraception with abortion and infanticide, and the Bishops of St Albans and Nassau were equally adamant that orthodox Christian doctrine had been undermined.[1] The bonds of affection and the unity of the Communion were tested. The temper of the times, though, was neither to unchurch minority opinion nor to confuse the boundaries of orthodox faith with divisions over the moral questions of the day.

Who were the bishops who could consider and pass such resolutions on matters of faith and practice? No Anglican bishop, no matter how legitimately consecrated, has ever possessed any *right* to attend a Lambeth Conference. From the first, these Conferences have assembled as the consequence of a series of personal invitations.

In 1867 there was no doubt that it was the Archbishop of Canterbury himself who would do the inviting and determine who should come. So it has remained. In 1867 Longley included on his invitation list the (then relatively few) retired Anglican bishops. No subsequent Archbishop has thought fit to do so. Now it would seem entirely impractical on numerical grounds alone, though once that was thought to rule out suffragans and assistant bishops let alone spouses, all of whom are now involved. In recent decades successive Archbishops of Canterbury have refused to invite the bishops of the Church of England in South Africa,[2] despite extensive lobbying on their behalf. In 1988 Sudanese bishops illegally consecrated by the previous Primate of that Province after his (unwilling) retirement arrived in Canterbury uninvited. They were swiftly despatched without a media storm or anyone much being aware of them. The refusal of Rowan Williams to invite (at least initially) to the 2008 Conference either the Bishop of New Hampshire, the Bishop of Harare, or any of the bishops consecrated in North America by African primates simply continues a practice established by his predecessors.

In 1867 there was one Anglican bishop who received no invitation, John William Colenso. Born in Cornwall and later the incumbent of Forncett St Mary in the Diocese of Norwich, he became the Bishop of Natal. He had been deposed by his metropolitan Robert Gray, the Bishop of Cape Town. An appeal to the Judicial Committee of the Privy Council had reinstated Colenso. Despite this, Longley excluded Colenso from his invitation list. In any case, Gray would not have Colenso back. He wanted to establish the independent competence in matters of discipline of each colonial church and also wanted their acts recognised as authoritative throughout the Anglican Communion. Gray had originally appointed Colenso but lived to regret it. Colenso's speeches, sermons, and theological writings moved beyond what was then considered orthodox. He questioned the historical reliability and accuracy of the Old Testament and was a champion of indigenous African culture, all of which may suggest he was a man before his time. But he was more of a mathematician than a theologian. While he stumbled across some now widely accepted views, his manner of arguing for them was neither subtle nor winning.[3] By the time the Lambeth Conference met the well-esteemed Vicar of Wantage, William John Butler, was bishop-elect of Natal but the decision of the Privy Council had prevented his consecration. Gray wanted Butler to be invited to the Lambeth Conference and the deposition of Colenso to be formally recognised. Such matters about who was or who was not a bishop were, according to Gray, matters of faith, and not second-order issues.

News of the trouble in South Africa had earlier reached Canada, where the bishops of the United Church of England and Ireland in Canada, meeting in Synod in Montreal in December 1865, expressed their concern. They believed that the age in which they lived was a very troubled one in the Anglican Communion. That's why they asked the Archbishop of Canterbury 'to convene a national synod of the bishops of the Anglican Church at home and abroad'.

From the perspective of the present day the 1860s seems a period when the Church of England, let alone the Anglican Communion, was settled, growing, and confident. Yet many at the time thought it was a period of deep religious uncertainty. The previous decade had ended with the publication of *Essays and Reviews*. Unexceptionable (and barely readable) now, this book generated great controversy. Half of all Church of England clergy eventually stirred themselves sufficiently to sign a petition of protest, a unique event in Anglican history. They wanted the world to know that, contrary to the opinions of the authors of *Essays and Reviews*, they maintained 'without reserve or qualification' that the punishment of the wicked, like the life of the righteous, was everlasting.[4] The petition illustrates how deep went the anxiety about what was thought to be the collapse of orthodox doctrine at the time. There were other anxieties too. The restoration of the Roman Catholic hierarchy in England and Wales a decade before had led to a new confidence among Roman Catholics. Methodism, though frequently afflicted by denominational division, continued to grow. And the forces of unbelief in England were becoming more insistent and even respectable. These anxieties had their echoes elsewhere in the world.

It was the unthreatening yet prescient leadership of Charles Longley as Archbishop of Canterbury that made the Lambeth Conference a possibility. He sensed intuitively that the time was right. The steamship had made a world-wide conference a possibility and a practicality. It was no accident that the First Vatican Council was called in 1870. A similar dynamic applied. The world began to feel smaller. What happened in Africa caused anxiety in Canada and had repercussions in India and Australia. (The Internet has given international theological controversy even more immediacy in our own age.) Even imperial authority was far from the cohesive factor for the Anglican Communion often presumed and more a problem to be solved. If the Anglican Communion was not governed from Canterbury or Westminster wherein lay any source of authority for solving its problems and divisions? The very first Lambeth Conference was the consequence of this dilemma rather than an illustration of the solidarity of a world-wide church, then amply demonstrated, and now disintegrating.

In 1867 Archbishop Longley coped with bishops refusing his invitation with remarkable equanimity. He didn't overplay his hand. It now seems to us self-evident that the Archbishop of Canterbury holds a primacy of honour within the Anglican Communion. It was not so self-evident at a practical level in the mid-nineteenth century. It was true that the Canadian bishops specifically asked the Archbishop of Canterbury to convene a world-wide conference, since they perceived no one else had the antiquity of office and honour which Cantuar possessed. Within England, however, the distinction between the Primate of England (the Archbishop of York) and the Primate of all England (the Archbishop of Canterbury) was one over which there was great sensitivity in the northern Province. The very acceptance of an invitation to the Lambeth Conference might suggest a superior authority, one of the reasons that made Archbishop Thomson of York so unlikely to attend. The Bishop of London was also inclined to consider that he had a particular connection with the Church of England overseas. The first Anglican churches in the United States, as well as Anglican churches within continental Europe, either had been or remained under the episcopal care of the Bishop of London rather than the Archbishop of Canterbury. Archibald Campbell Tait, Bishop of London at the time of the first Lambeth Conference, was not the sort to neglect colonial issues or to feel that he could only act through the Archbishop of Canterbury in addressing them.

Following the decision of the Judicial Committee of the Privy Council in his favour, Bishop Colenso had brought an action to secure the continuance of the income that he had received as Bishop of Natal from the Colonial Bishoprics Fund. This had been withheld as a consequence of his deposition. In November 1866 the Master of the Rolls, Lord Romilly, gave judgment in Colenso's favour, though in such a way that it made the legal status of colonial bishoprics even more confusing. A change of government brought Lord Carnarvon to the Colonial Office. He planned fresh legislation for the following year. Tait asked the Archbishop of Canterbury if he would send a letter to all the colonial churches inviting their bishops (and their synods of clergy) to say what they wanted. Longley refused. So the Bishop of London took it upon himself to write in October 1866 to all bishops, deans, and archdeacons in the Anglican Communion.[5] He said that he wanted to be in accurate possession of the views of members of colonial churches since he was likely to take a very active part in parliamentary deliberations on forthcoming legislation affecting them. He put four questions, asking those to whom he wrote to ascertain the views of both clergy and laity in their dioceses before responding.

1 Should all bishops in the British colonies take an oath of canonical obedience to the Archbishop of Canterbury?
2 Should there be any appeal against the decisions of bishops or synods in the colonial churches to any authority at home, and if so what?
3 How could the royal supremacy be maintained in the colonial churches?
4 What seems the best guarantee for maintaining unity of doctrine and discipline between the different scattered branches of our church?

Tait received somewhere around eighty substantial replies to this letter over the course of the next few months. The only indignant ones came from South Africa, and especially from the Bishop of Cape Town who was furious with this communication from a bishop with whom his diocese was not connected and addressing his clergy in such an impertinent fashion. Others were less sensitive, and Tait got what he wanted, namely assurances from a variety of colonial churchmen that they did not want to see links with the mother church in England or with the Crown severed. Government by the synods of their own churches or the unfettered rule of their own bishops did not always provide an attractive alternative to the establishment of the Church of England. But no one could quite identify what would be right. There was no consensus.

Lambeth 1867's Aftermath

This, then, was the context in which the first Lambeth Conference of bishops gathered in 1867. Uncertainty about authority, an episcopal scandal with all the consequent fall-out, unease about the signs of the times, a deep instinct that this world-wide Communion of churches needed some international forum to ensure unity in doctrine and discipline – the reason for a Lambeth Conference in 1867 seems a mirror image of the presenting issues in 2008. At the General Synod in July 2007, the Bishop of Durham, Tom Wright, said that the Anglican Communion had never previously faced the circumstances which required a novel development such as the Anglican Covenant. It seems gravely mistaken to assume Anglicanism has not travelled this way before. The rails of the Anglican train seem to have been set on much the same uncertain track for a century and a half. That it has not arrived at any final destination may simply be due to the very provisionality of the Anglican tradition.

In 1867 the problems would have been incapacitating if history had provided this Communion of churches simply with a British monarch who was supreme governor of only some of them. This Communion also possessed an

Archbishop with a pedigree even more historic than any
monarch of England and whose earliest predecessors pre-
sided over a united church in England well before England
was herself a united country. The Archbishop of Canterbury found himself the holder of an office with fresh utility
and symbolic significance in a new age.

If it became evident that the Archbishop could gather the
whole Anglican episcopate around him (the refuseniks from
the first Conference diminished considerably by the second), Longley and his successors nevertheless recognised
the limitations of their authority. They had no capacity to
coerce or compel. Theirs was the authority of a pastor and
teacher, whose credibility relied not simply upon antiquity
of office but in building bonds of affection.

In November 1887 when Archbishop Benson (whose
personality was scarcely devoid of a capacity to compel)
sent his letter of invitation to the third Lambeth Conference
he included among subjects to be discussed 'definite
teaching of the faith' and 'mutual relations of dioceses and
branches of the Anglican Communion'.[6] In the event the
report on 'definite teaching of the faith' was the only one to
remain unaccepted by the 1888 Conference and unpub-
lished. The failure to do so lay in the power of the controversies of the day (in this case questions related to the
theory of evolution) so to dominate minds that disagreement on second-order details gave the impression of much
deeper doctrinal division than actually existed. There was a
longing to agree too much: that continues to be an Anglican
Achilles' heel in our own age.

Benson died before the next Conference in 1897 but did
help to shape it, and some of the same themes resurfaced in
a bolder way. One resolution requested the Archbishop of
Canterbury to establish a consultative body 'to which resort

may be had, if desired, by the national churches, Provinces, and extra-provincial dioceses of the Anglican Communion either for information or advice'.[7] This was an idea which even then had a history. Bishop John Wordsworth of Salisbury (with some encouragement from Canterbury) had been part of a group of bishops who had proposed a consultative body and a court of reference in a paper published in 1895. As we have seen, only the consultative body made it as far as a Lambeth Conference resolution. Hopes remained, however, that once this body was established, something more authoritative would inevitably follow. At the time there was concern that very small Provinces did not have the theological or legislative resources they needed. Provincial autonomy was risky when a Province could be dominated by one or two powerful personalities whose opinions might well prove heterodox. Offer some advice, it was thought, and the consequent gratitude would lead eventually to the establishment of a body within the Anglican Communion which everyone would agree should have authority. Such a line of thought is discernible in the Windsor Report where the Council of Advice for the Archbishop of Canterbury has a surprisingly similar genesis and, when coupled with the proposal for an Anglican Covenant, entertains hopes for the development of binding Communion-wide authority.

Once the 1908 Conference was in prospect, Bishop John Wordsworth was disappointed. The consultative body had been established. It had met on more than one occasion but kept all its debates confidential and issued neither minutes nor recommendations much less any authoritative statement. The Court of Reference or tribunal now seemed an unlikely consequent innovation.

But the consultative body did not die. The 1908

Conference devoted no fewer than three resolutions to it, the first of which determined its composition (a membership of 18) in some detail. This suggestion of authority, however, was speedily modified by succeeding resolutions which said that the Central Consultative Body (as it was now to be called, the adjective at first appearing significant) must be careful not to overstep the mark by undermining provincial regulation or decide on anything not mentioned in the notice summoning members to the meeting. It would be hard to devise a more effective means of preventing this new Central Body from dealing with crises as they emerged. Even so, by 1920 that year's Conference solemnly proclaimed 'in order to prevent misapprehension the Conference declares that the Consultative Body created by the Lambeth Conference of 1897 and consolidated by the Conference of 1908, is a purely advisory body. It ... neither possesses nor claims any executive or administrative power. It is framed so as to represent all branches of the Anglican Communion and it offers advice only when advice is asked for.' Had it attempted too much?

The 1930 Conference passed a similar resolution about the Consultative Body (though the adjective 'Central' had by then disappeared). It also felt moved to resolve 'the formation of a central appellate tribunal to be inconsistent with the spirit of the Anglican Communion'. In 1948 the Consultative Body passed unmentioned in the resolutions but made a reappearance in 1958, when it was noted that it was 'of the nature of a continuation committee of the Lambeth conference'. In 1968 the Anglican Consultative Council was proposed and subsequently established, creating something significantly different to a continuation committee of the Lambeth Conference, but still a very long way from the sort of authoritative tribunal dreamed of by

Bishop John Wordsworth towards the end of the previous century.

This reluctance to submit to central government in Anglicanism has not prevented a predilection for international gatherings. Anglicans like international conferences even if they don't much care for universal jurisdiction. Many have observed a deficiency here. It was trenchantly expressed towards the end of the 1988 Lambeth Conference.

There is a vacuum at the centre of the Anglican Communion where hard decisions affecting the entire body are to be taken. The Lambeth Conference is not a legislative assembly or a church council. It is not a tribunal. It has no jurisdiction. Neither history, nor the present mind of the churches that supply it give it authority beyond the considerable moral authority inherent in a large congregation of bishops.[8]

So said an editorial in *The Tablet*. Since so much of the 1988 Conference concentrated on unity and authority within the Anglican Communion this observation from a source often so sympathetic to Anglicanism touched some episcopal raw nerves. The weakness of Lambeth Conferences has not been a lack of teaching or the failure to produce substantial recommendations or reports. These have frequently been of considerable quality given the limited resources available to the bishops and the timeframe for their production. The weakness lies in a peculiar unwillingness of Provinces and their bishops to consider these resolutions and reports subsequently by debating and discussing them in their own synods and assemblies. This limits the effective authority of the Lambeth bishops and diminishes what could be a much more significant way of enabling local churches to relate to the wider Communion. A concentration on isolated resolutions makes the matter worse. Demands that Resolution 1.10 on human sexuality from the 1998 Lambeth Conference should be automatically treated as authoritative throughout the Communion have proved unconvincing because of the inattention paid to the other hundred or so resolutions from the same Conference, let alone all those from earlier Conferences. If there has been a fault in the Anglican Communion over the past 150 years it has not been a dearth of episcopal teaching at the international level. There has been, however, a serious failure across the Provinces, especially in the last generation, to consider and ingest this teaching, a failure in which the bishops themselves have too often been complicit. The related causes and consequences are now serious, but not entirely beyond remedy.

What of Today?

Where do we go from here? There does indeed seem to be far too little interest in the history of the Anglican Communion and why it has developed in its present form. Hensley Henson, sometime Bishop of Durham, once referred to the organisation of the Anglican Communion as 'a subject of portentous dullness'.[9] Too often bishops and others have acquiesced in this assessment for fear of being thought dull themselves. But not to know our own history is a serious shortcoming for Anglicans, for whom history and theology are inseparable. It is historical circumstances, after all, which mean that Anglicanism is a communion of churches rather than a single world-wide Church in itself. These Anglican churches have different polities, a consequence of their history and social context. Sometimes their history has been shaped by the theological tradition within Anglicanism which nurtured them through the activities of various missionary societies. Anglicanism's development internationally is surprising because it had fewer elements of empire than seems commonly assumed.

It was the very complexity of its relationship with the state which meant that the Church of England could not submit to any higher international authority, the cause of so much English discontent in 1867. When the bishops of the Church of England were asked to consecrate an American priest as a bishop in 1784 they were extremely cautious, and in the end refused. Establishing a branch of the Church of England beyond England and in a setting where the Crown had no jurisdiction made them reluctant. While consecrations of overseas bishops were soon to become commonplace in Lambeth Palace chapel, the history of the development of the Anglican Communion is not one of wholesale subjection to English authority. Missionaries from England were often at work in foreign places well before British rule was established or even contemplated. The Anglican record in seeking to establish indigenous churches in such places as Madagascar or East and West Africa is a notable one. It was later, towards the end of the nineteenth century, that a more imperialist perspective began to dominate, one which identified European traditions with Christian civilisation itself. Bill Jacob's seminal work on the history of the Anglican Communion which gives an excellent account of these developments deserves much greater Communion-wide study than it has received.[10] There has been a Communion-wide failure to take our own history seriously or seek to understand it. It is little wonder that we fail to comprehend why our churches differ so much or why they view the Communion itself in such contrasting ways.

There is, moreover, another serious consequence of this failure to disseminate the breadth of teaching from Lambeth Conferences. Our Communion fails to recognise how doctrine develops and Christian practice changes in relation to surrounding culture and new learning. Bishops at the most recent Lambeth Conferences seem to have been largely unaware of what their predecessors have resolved and taught. It seems a strange state of affairs for those who are bearers of tradition themselves.

Intriguingly it was the first Archbishop of Nigeria, Timothy Olufosoye, who commented at a meeting of African bishops in 1987 that many of the topics proposed for the Lambeth Conference the following year had already been the subject of many earlier Lambeth resolutions. It was his gentle prompting which caused all resolutions of previous Lambeth Conferences to be collated into a single handbook. This was made available to members of the Steering Committee of the 1988 Lambeth Conference. The generality of the Conference membership, however, did not possess this resource. But such a collection of resolutions was found so useful that it was later published, in 1992.[11] The resolutions of the 1988 Conference were added, along with a magisterial essay by Owen Chadwick. It was hoped this would provide essential reading for those who would gather for the 1998 Lambeth Conference. I recall no reference of any sort in 1998 to this major work. Very few were the bishops who seemed aware of this publication. Perhaps it was not surprising therefore that with the exception of those on ecumenism very few 1998 Lambeth resolutions make any reference to reports, documents, or resolutions from earlier Lambeth Conferences. Two particularly striking examples of this collective episcopal amnesia occurred in relation to the resolutions on war and human sexuality.

Resolution 1.4 ('A Faithful Response to Aggression and War') was notable for a total absence of any biblical or doctrinal reference. The 1998 Lambeth Conference was the first to fail to reaffirm the statement of the 1930 Lambeth bishops that 'war as a method of settling international disputes is incompatible with the teaching and example of our Lord Jesus Christ'. No one seemed to notice this omission. Collectively the bishops appeared content with much vaguer statements deploring war in general but not grounded in historic Anglican teaching which sought to be a faithful interpretation of the mind of Christ. In 1998 immense priority was given to the collective opinions of the present day.

Resolution 1.10 from the 1998 Conference also made no reference of any sort to earlier Lambeth teaching on marriage and sexuality, despite a large, impressive, and often influential amount of material on these matters. By contrast, when the 1968 Conference met, the continuing and world-wide debate following the papal encyclical *Humanae Vitae* was a major preoccupation. The Lambeth bishops looked to their predecessors as well as to Scripture and themselves for guidance. They declared themselves unable to agree with the papal disapproval of all methods of artificial contraception, or that it was always contrary to 'the order established by God'. Rather impressively, the 1968 Conference then went on to reaffirm in considerable detail the teaching of its 1958 predecessor. The theological and ethical wheels did not require reinvention but renewed application. This strong sense of building the teaching from one Lambeth Conference to the next disappeared almost without trace in 1998. Such slippage from the moorings of cumulative teaching is one of the sources of our contemporary malaise. What is strange is that it took place so decisively at precisely the time when the Lambeth bishops were convinced that they were reaffirming an unchanging tradition, especially in the area of human sexuality.

Perhaps to the surprise of many it now seems almost forgotten that the 1978 and 1988 Conferences also passed resolutions on homosexuality. The resolution in 1988 seems very distant in tone and content from what was passed a decade later and yet it was firmly located within historic Christian teaching and built on established teaching.

This Conference:

1   Reaffirms the statement of the Lambeth Conference of 1978 on homosexuality, recognising the continuing need in the next decade for 'deep and dispassionate study of the question of homosexuality, which would take seriously both the teaching of Scripture and the results of scientific and medical research'.

2   Urges such study and reflection to take account of biological, genetic and psychological research being undertaken by other agencies, and the sociocultural factors that lead to the different attitudes in the provinces of our Communion.

3   Calls each province to reassess, in the light of such study and because of our concern for human rights, its care for and attitude towards persons of homosexual orientation.

This resolution from a decade earlier passed without any mention at all in the report of the 1998 Lambeth Conference.

The troubles that have afflicted the Anglican Communion over the past decade have made many people impatient with the Lambeth Conference method of passing resolutions. What's the point, ask some, if they are not going to be obeyed? What's the necessity, ask others, if this simply gives the majority a stick with which to compel and exclude minorities? Why not instead create a Communion-wide space for episcopal fellowship and, if possible, the same international experience for clergy and laity as well? Surely if we simply study the Scriptures, pray, and worship together, this will help forge a path towards a renewed and unified Communion?

Bishops have returned from the last two Lambeth Conferences testifying that the best experience for them was found in the intimacy of the Bible study groups and the personal exchange of stories and experiences with their colleagues. The 2008 Conference seems to be planned even more explicitly as a retreat, a prayer gathering, and a Bible study on a grand scale. It may prove to be neither a Council nor a Synod nor even a Conference. If so, that would be a loss of nerve and a failure to keep faith with one of our most significant instruments of Communion. We need to resolve to confer before we can confer to resolve anything. The Council of Jerusalem (Acts 15) would not have been possible had this principle not been followed. A Communion-wide conference remains the best means to recover the cumulative teaching ability of the Anglican Communion itself. The authority of such teaching can only be found in its reception by Anglican churches as a whole, of course, but God has given us the means of such unity.

There is no one likely to replace the Archbishop of Canterbury as the legitimate convenor of a world-wide Anglican conference of bishops. We are fortunate that our present Archbishop is little tempted to coerce or compel but maintains a strong commitment to the value of the invitation to confer. Like Archbishop Longley in 1867, it would be wise not to be too disturbed by episcopal refu-seniks. Perhaps most of all, however, the bishops who gather for Lambeth in 2008 need fresh induction into their own history and tradition. It is a teaching tradition which gains authority by dissemination in the Communion as a whole and by being reworked every decade. In 1867 a tradition was established through conferring rather than governing which gave life and shape to a world-wide Communion of episcopal churches. It has not yet com-pleted its work.

Notes

1 H. Hensley Henson, *Retrospect of an Unimportant Life, Vol 2* (Oxford: University Press, 1943), pp. 273–5.
2 This evangelical and reformed body traces its origin back to disruption in the South African Church in 1870 and was orga-nised in its present form in 1938.
3 For an account of these matters see Alan Stephenson, *The First Lambeth Conference 1867* (London: SPCK, 1967) and his further volume, *Anglicanism and the Lambeth Conferences* (London: SPCK, 1978).
4 See Owen Chadwick, *The Victorian Church, Vol 2* (London: A & C Black, 2nd edn, 1972), pp. 75–97.
5 R. T. Davidson and W. Benham, *Life of Archibald Campbell Tait, Vol 1* (London: MacMillan, 1891), pp. 365ff.
6 See R. T. Davidson, (ed.), *The Lambeth Conferences of 1867, 1878, 1888* (London: SPCK, 1889).

7 For all Lambeth Conference resolutions see Roger Coleman (ed.) *Resolutions of the twelve Lambeth Conferences 1867–1988* (Toronto: Anglican Book Centre, 1992).

8 *The Tablet*, 6 August 1988.

9 Henson, *Retrospect, Vol 2*, p. 277.

10 W. M. Jacob, *The Making of the Anglican Church Worldwide* (London: SPCK, 1997). See also Kevin Ward, *A History of Global Anglicanism* (Cambridge University Press, 2006).

11 See Coleman, *Resolutions*, above.

6

Norman Doe[1]

Common Principles of Canon Law in Anglicanism

Although the 44 member churches of the Anglican Communion are in communion with the See of Canterbury, each church is autonomous, free to govern itself according to its own legal system.[2] Within each institutional church, general law (typically provincial) is created by a synod or other assembly representative of bishops, clergy, and laity, and laws made at more localised levels (such as diocesan law created by the diocesan synod of bishop, clergy, and laity) must be consistent with the general law.[3] Some churches have a code of canons only.[4] Most have a constitution, canons, and other regulatory instruments,[5] including: rules and regulations,[6] ordinances,[7] resolutions,[8] and liturgical rubrics found in the service books.[9] Alongside written laws are less formal and sometimes unwritten sources: customs or tradition,[10] the decisions of church courts,[11] the English Canons Ecclesiastical 1603,[12] or pre-Reformation Roman canon law.[13] Whereas offices and institutions exist at the global level of the Anglican Communion, namely, the instruments of unity and communion (Archbishop of Canterbury, Lambeth Conference,

Primates' Meeting, and Anglican Consultative Council), there is no body at this level competent to make decisions binding on individual churches.[14] There is no body of global law in Anglicanism: the decisions of the institutional instruments of unity have persuasive moral authority not enforceable juridical authority, unless incorporated in the laws of member churches. Rather, ecclesial communion in Anglicanism is maintained by non-juridical 'bonds of affection'.[15] However, recent tensions in the Communion have stimulated discussion of the meaning and limits of the bonds of affection. This has led to exploration of ways in which the laws of churches may contribute to more visible global ecclesial communion in Anglicanism.[16]

Background

In March 2001, at Kanuga, North Carolina, USA, on the basis of a paper discussed at the event,[17] the Primates' Meeting decided to explore whether there is an unwritten common law shared by the member churches of the Communion. A Legal Advisers' Consultation met in Canterbury in March 2002, to test the hypothesis. The Consultation formulated six conclusions:

1 There are principles of canon law common to the churches of the Anglican Communion;
2 Their existence can be factually established;
3 Each Province or church contributes through its own legal system to the principles of canon law common within the Communion;
4 These principles have strong persuasive authority and are fundamental to the self-understanding of each of the member churches;

5 These principles have a living force, and contain
   within themselves the possibility for further development; and
6 The existence of the principles both demonstrates and
   promotes unity in the Communion.[18]

At Canterbury in April 2002, the Primates' Meeting discussed a report on the Consultation and concluded: 'The
Primates recognised that the unwritten law common to the
Churches of the Communion and expressed as shared
principles of canon law may be understood to constitute a
fifth "instrument of unity".' The Meeting also endorsed the
suggestion to establish a network of lawyers to work on a
draft statement of the principles. Subsequently, at Hong
Kong in September 2002 the Anglican Consultative
Council welcomed the establishment of a Network of
Anglican Legal Advisers to: (a) produce a statement of
principles of canon law common within the Communion;
(b) examine shared legal problems and possible solutions;
and (c) provide reports to the Joint Standing Committee of
the Primates' Meeting and the Anglican Consultative
Council as the work progresses. In October 2003, the Primates' Meeting urged completion of the work, as did the
Lambeth Commission in its *Windsor Report* (2004).[19] A
drafting group of the Legal Advisers' Network met in
Toronto (October 2005) and Nassau (April 2006) to work
on drafts of the statement, and meetings of the full Network
are scheduled for late in 2007 in order to finalise the
statement (prior to the Lambeth Conference in 2008).

The Legal Advisers' Consultation, at Canterbury 2002,
examined forty-four candidate principles formulated prior
to the event, of which it agreed forty-three[20]; the exercise
was to determine whether these principles surface explicitly

or implicitly in the laws of the churches. What follows is an explanation of each of its six conclusions.

1. There are principles of canon law common to the churches within the Anglican Communion

The category 'the principles of canon law' is already formally recognised by at least four Anglican churches: the Provinces of the West Indies,[21] Southern Africa,[22] Central Africa,[23] and Nigeria.[24] It is also recognised by other traditions.[25] Many churches in the Communion explicitly appeal to principles in their own legal systems,[26] as the foundation for more detailed rules, giving the latter shape, coherence, meaning, and purpose. Principles of canon law tend to be in the nature of general propositions or maxims which express fundamental ecclesial values; some are descriptive,[27] others prescriptive.[28] Principles differ from *rules* (which apply to specific circumstances) and enjoy 'a dimension of weight'.[29] They may also articulate theological values.[30] But some principles may have no obvious theological dimension, and may indeed be shared with secular legal systems, such as the principle that individuals should not be inflicted with penalties except in accordance with law.[31] Many are rooted in the inherited canonical tradition,[32] in its various forms.[33]

2. The existence of the principles can be factually established

The principles of canon law common to the churches are induced from the factual coincidences of actual laws of each church. Their recognition is a scientific task. There are, as a matter of fact, profound similarities between the laws of Anglican churches: identifying the similarities is merely an exercise in careful observation based on a comparison of legal texts, juxtaposing one with another. Often legal similarities are generated by the churches using a common historical source, such as a Lambeth Conference resolution,[34] or rubrics of the Book of Common Prayer 1662.[35] From these similarities emerge shared general principles. For instance: from similar rules on 'excommunication', 'suspension', 'exclusion', or 'repulsion' from Holy Communion, may be induced the principle that eucharistic discipline is ultimately in the keeping of the bishop.[36] The theological basis for exclusion may be found in Scripture,[37] and doctrine[38]; and the historical antecedents of the principle are rooted in the canonical tradition.[39] The similarities of texts on excommunication produce a general proposition, which underscores a fundamental ecclesial value.[40]

3. Each church contributes through its own legal system to the principles of canon law common within the Communion

The Anglican *ius commune*, as the collective effect of similarities between legal systems, is not imposed from above. The immanence of common principles in actual legal similarities means that each Anglican church is the legislator of the *ius commune*. Whenever a church legislates, it contributes to the *ius commune* and its law may function as a precedent for other churches. While churches are autonomous, as a matter of practice they often adopt or adapt provisions in the legal systems of fellow churches.[41] The adoption of the same rule by other churches adds to the store of similarities, and, in turn, these similarities generate a common principle. For example: Canon 21 of the Fourth Lateran Council 1215 forbids priests to breach the seal of the confessional; this general principle is repeated by the Church of England in Canon 113 of the 1603 Canons; and it is adopted by the Province of Southern Africa in its

Prayer Book 1989. Successive unilateral legislative adop-
tions by churches might themselves augment the authority
of the principle.

4. The principles have a strong persuasive authority and are fundamental to the self-understanding of each church in the Communion

The principles common to the churches of the Communion
have the appearance of laws (they may be preceptive, pro-
hibitive, or permissive), but they are not themselves laws:
they are principles of law.[42] 'Laws' are found in the
enforceable instruments (constitutions etc) of each institutional church; the principles of canon law are derived from
laws and are not binding locally unless the laws of that
church permit this.[43] Laws which enable, for instance,
participation of the laity in government tell us a great deal
about the Anglican understanding of representative ecclesiastical polity (as compared for example with Roman
Catholicism).[44] Often, laws of churches themselves portray
a principle as having a deeper authority, beyond that of the
formal law in which it appears, through its antiquity or its
underlying spiritual origin. For example: the law of the
former Church of India, Pakistan, Burma, and Ceylon
provides that the church 'has received the principles and
customs set out in the ... Declarations from the Holy
Catholic Church of ages past'; moreover, the church
'believes that it was by the guidance of the Holy Spirit that
those principles came to be recognised and those customs
adopted'.[45]

5. The principles have a living force, and contain in themselves the possibility of further development

The idea here is that each church through its own legislative activity may contribute to or subtract from the store of principles, particularly when such developments are replicated around the Communion. For example: churches are increasingly legislating to forbid racial discrimination in the membership and government of the church[46]; also, churches are developing rules on the admission of the unconfirmed to Holy Communion, particularly children.[47] Such examples may indicate the evolutionary character of the *ius commune* of the Anglican Communion.[48] Moreover, differences, and arguably conflicts, between the details of laws are in the nature of conditions under which shared principles are applied. The principles are shared; differences exist with regard to their detailed application in each church.[49] For example: laws vary as to the grounds for exclusion from Holy Communion; these include: 'living in grievous sin' (England); 'malice and hatred' (Canada); 'bringing the church into disrepute' (Wales) and 'indictable offences' (West Indies). The laws of all churches spell out the grounds for exclusion. While the grounds vary, the principle of exclusion from communion is common to all churches.

6. The existence of the principles both demonstrates unity and promotes unity within the Anglican Communion

The Anglican *ius commune* might be perceived by some as a threat to the autonomy of the member churches, or that it could contribute to global divisions.[50] However, the *ius commune* is itself a product of the exercise of the autonomy of churches and of their promotion of communion through their contributions to it. Their autonomy, which may be understood as manifested in the principles they have generated, is unaffected: churches remain free juridically to depart from them. Indeed, that legal systems converge in shared principles of canon law common to the churches is a concrete expression of the very character of Anglicanism and its understanding of church. The collective effect of the similarities between individual canonical systems is a major contribution both to Anglican identity and cohesion. The principles indicate concretely the unity Anglicans share at global level and their elucidation affirms the integrity of the values reflected in them. Moreover, recognition that individual churches contribute to the *ius commune* underscores their own individual responsibility for the shape and maintenance of Anglican identity. An understanding of first principles may also be a useful resource for churches seeking to reform and develop their own legal systems.[51]

The Drafting Process and Text

The Legal Advisers' Consultation 2002 agreed broadly (but was not overly exercised by the issue) that a number of tests may be formulated to establish whether a principle of canon law is one common to the churches:

1   *The Unanimity Test*: Does the principle appear in the laws of all Anglican churches? For example: in all churches, candidates for admission to the office of diocesan bishop must be elected to that office.[52] And/or:

2   *The Majority Test*: Does the principle appear in the laws of a majority of Anglican churches? For example: a minister duly ordained as priest or deacon may officiate in a diocese after receiving authority to do so from the diocesan bishop.[53] And/or:

3   *The Face Validity Test*: Is the principle accepted by
     most Anglican churches though it is not expressly
     found in their laws? For example: later laws abrogate
     earlier laws. And/or:

4   *The Reversal Test*: If the principle was reversed would
     that reversed proposition be accepted as not being
     part of the Anglican *ius commune*? For example: the
     unacceptability of the proposition that 'assistant
     bishops are not subordinate to the overriding jur-
     isdiction of the diocesan bishop' would suggest that
     the proposition 'assistant bishops are subject to their
     commissioning bishop' is a principle of Anglican
     common law.[54] And/or:

5   *The Common Source Test*: Can the principle be traced
     back to a common, historical source even when some
     legal systems may be silent on the matter? For
     example: clergy must obey the lawful commands of
     their bishops.[55] And/or:

6   *The Canonical Tradition Test*: Can the principle be
     traced back to or does it equate with a principle of the
     canonical tradition? For example: priests and dea-
     cons must not engage in any occupations or habits
     which are inconsistent with their sacred calling.[56]
     And/or:

7   *The Fundamental Ecclesial Value Test*: Is the principle
     a general, foundational proposition expressing a basic
     ecclesial value, even if it does not appear in the for-
     mal laws of all churches? For example: a priest must
     not disclose information received in the confes-
     sional.[57] And/or:

8   *The Theological Dimension Test*: If the principle has
     explicitly or implicitly a distinctive theological
     dimension, then it may be part of the common law.

For example: confirmation is validly administered by the Episcopal laying on of hands. And/or:

9 *The Perception Test*: is the principle understood as one held in common with fellow churches of the Communion? For example: there should be no discrimination in the membership and government of a church.[58] And/or:

10 *The Reconciliation Test*: Are the differences or conflicts between the rules of a minority of churches reconcilable? For example: in some churches, such as the Church in Wales, deposition from holy orders is reversible but in others, such as the Church of Nigeria, it is not; yet all churches operate the principle that clergy may be lawfully deposed in appropriate cases. And/or:

11 *The Global Consensus Test*: Would the breach of the principle result in a substantial risk of serious division at the global level of the Communion?

An initial draft statement of one hundred principles was placed on the website of the Anglican Communion Network of Legal Advisers in the summer of 2005. It was this draft which was considered by the Network group in Toronto (2005) and Nassau (2006) and this awaits formal discussion by the full Network late in 2007.[59] This draft text provides: 'A "principle of canon law" is a foundational proposition or maxim of general applicability which has a strong dimension of weight, is induced from the similarities of the legal systems of churches, derives from the canonical tradition or other practices of the church, expresses a basic theological truth or ethical value, and is about, is implicit in, or underlies canon law.'[60]

The hundred principles are arranged in the draft under

eight Parts; each of the hundred macro-principles consists of micro-principles, of which there are approximately six hundred and fifty. Part I, 'Order in the Church', deals with the necessity for law in ecclesial society, the role of law as the servant of the church, the conditional nature of church law, the sources, subjects, and forms of church law, the rule of law in the church, the requirement of authority, the effect and application of law, and the interpretation of law.[61] Part II is concerned with 'The Anglican Communion' and includes principles relating to the nature of the Communion, the Instruments of Unity, the freedom of self-governance of each church, mutual respect between churches, juridical presumptions, and the mutual availability of ministrations.[62] Principles of 'Ecclesiastical Government' in Part III are on: polity, leadership and authority, administration, delegation, representative church government, legislative competence, legislation, lay participation in church government, visitations of a supervisory jurisdiction or a pastoral ministry, and judicial process in courts and tribunals.[63]

Part IV consists of principles of 'Ministry', such as the principle of the three-fold ordained ministry of bishops, priests, and deacons, public ministry as service, the professional ethic of public ministry, the exercise of office, the office of Primate, archbishops and metropolitical authority, admission to the episcopate, ministry of diocesan bishops, assistant bishops, the ordination of priests and deacons, authority to minister in a diocese, ministry common to priests and deacons, the ministry of priests with care of souls, the ministry of deacons, pastoral care and availability, termination of ordained ministry, the role of the laity, classes and rolls of church membership, rights and duties of the faithful, lay ministers and officers in the church, and professional and personal relationships in ministry.[64] 'Doctrine and Liturgy' are treated in Part V, including principles on doctrine and profession of the faith, the sources of doctrine, the development of doctrine, preaching, teaching, and outreach, theological differences and freedom of conscience, doctrinal discipline, public worship and liturgy, the making and authorisation of forms of service, the administration of public worship, the provision of public worship, choice of alternative forms of service, control over public worship, and liturgical discipline.[65]

Principles relating to the major rites of passage (baptism, confirmation, marriage, and burial) as well as principles concerning rituals such as Holy Communion, confession, and exorcism can be found in Part VI, 'The Rites of the Church'.[66] Part VII contains principles relating to 'Church Property' including ownership and administration of church property, church buildings, and other places of worship, clergy residences, the keeping of ecclesiastical registers and records, the principle of stewardship, ministers' standards in relation to finance, the distribution and control of funds, sources of income, investments, insurance, and clergy stipends and pensions.[67] The final section, Part VIII on 'Ecumenical Relations', features principles relating to ecumenical responsibilities, freedom, recognition, agreement, collaboration, admission, and reception as well as the admission of non-Anglicans to Holy Communion.[68]

Other than the sections on church order,[69] and the Anglican Communion,[70] the grouping of principles into the eight Parts is conditioned by the systematisation of laws employed by the member churches, treating as they do ecclesiastical governance, ministry, doctrine and liturgy, ecclesiastical rites, church property and, increasingly, ecumenical relations.[71] The draft statement of principles is not

exhaustive. It omits, for example, civil law principles which
are often incorporated into church laws, such as the doctrine of consensual compact as the basis upon which
ecclesiastical jurisdiction is founded and exercised in most
secular legal systems[72]; the detailed procedures of church
assemblies[73]; or specialist ministries.[74] However, it would be
possible to formulate principles on such subjects.

A variety of sources is employed from which the principles are derived. Most are from church constitutions and
canons,[75] many from service books (which themselves enjoy
canonical authority), and their liturgical norms.[76] A great
number come from historical sources (the authority of
which may be canonically recognised or adopted by the
laws of churches), such as the Book of Common Prayer
1662,[77] the canonical tradition,[78] or from divine law,[79] or
the practice of the church universal.[80] Others are rooted in a
theological idea expressed in laws,[81] or are derived from
guidance issued by ecclesiastical authorities to supplement
and explain church law.[82] While the vast majority of the
principles derive from similarities between the written laws
of churches, some are based on unwritten assumptions,
general propositions implicit in church laws.[83] The juridical
values of clarity, conciseness, and consistency govern the
form of the principles, which themselves are cast in a variety
of different juridical formulae: most are permissions
('may'),[84] many are precepts ('shall', 'must'),[85] some are
prohibitions ('shall not', 'no one shall')[86]; many are
exhortations ('should'), expressing aspirational norms,[87]
and some are in the form of maxims ('is').[88]

The Anglican Project in Context

It is instructive to compare this Anglican project with the approaches of other international ecclesial communities to global ecclesiastical order. The following does so in relation to five matters: nature (and form); subject-matter; purpose; theological basis; and enforceability. While no other global ecclesial community has engaged in a project similar to that of the Anglican *ius commune* (articulating principles induced from the similarities of the laws of their member churches), their instruments fall into three basic categories: codes of canon law (Roman Catholic and Eastern Catholic); customs (Orthodox, canonical tradition); and constitutions (Lutheran, Reformed, Methodist, and Baptist) and statutes (Old Catholics in the Union of Utrecht).[89]

Nature and form

The Anglican *ius commune*, as a collection of principles, is similar to the code of the Latin or Roman Catholic Church, but different insofar as the former is generated from the grass roots by the legislative activity of the member churches of the Communion, whereas the latter is derived from a central authority, the papacy. The Latin Code of Canon Law 1983 was promulgated by Pope John Paul II after a revision process following the Second Vatican Council. As 'universal law', the code (along with papal decrees, and authentic interpretations of a legislator – judicial decisions do generate law),[90] applies to the Latin Church in all parts of the world. The Anglican *ius commune* seems to resemble a little more the Code of Canons of the Eastern Churches, the twenty-one oriental churches reunited with and acknowledging the supremacy of the Roman Pontiff. Promulgated by Pope John Paul II in 1990,[91] the code, in which 'the ancient law of the Eastern Churches has been mostly received or adapted', represents their 'common law': it embraces 'the laws and legitimate customs' of the entire Church and those common to all the Eastern Churches.[92]

Like the Anglican Communion, the Orthodox Church is a family of self-governing churches with no centralised organisation.[93] It has no universal code. The 'law of the church' globally is, rather, 'her canonical tradition', 'an outgrowth of the holy canons'.[94] The holy canons stem from three main sources: ecumenical synods (representing the universal church), local synods (subsequently ratified by the ecumenical synods as representing the tradition of the universal church), and the Fathers of the church. These are contained in several collections; the most widely used today in Greek-speaking Orthodox churches is the *Pedalion*.[95] Nevertheless, some Orthodox churches may at the inter-church level organise themselves on the basis of a *constitution*, such as that of the Standing Conference of Canonical Orthodox Bishops in the Americas.[96] No attempt has been made to articulate what such instruments share, though whether Orthodox law should be codified is the subject of debate.[97] Unlike the Anglican *ius commune*, the *constitutions* of other global ecclesial communities are not an articulation of principles induced in ascending fashion from similarities between the regulatory instruments of their member churches. They are, rather, instruments *de novo* enabling world-wide collaboration in matters of common concern,[98] while preserving the autonomy of member churches: the Lutheran World Federation is 'organized under' its constitution (and supplementary bylaws) as an 'instrument of its autonomous member churches'[99]; the World Alliance of Reformed Churches adopted its present constitution in 1970[100]; the World Methodist Council has a constitution but the Council has no legislative authority over member churches[101]; and the Baptist World Alliance has a constitution which 'recognizes the traditional autonomy and interdependence of Baptist churches and member bodies'.[102]

Subject-matter

There is considerable but not exact convergence between global ecclesial communities as to the subjects treated by their regulatory instruments. The Latin code is comprehensive and treats: general norms; the people of God; the teaching office; the sanctifying office (the sacraments); temporal goods; sanctions; and processes.[103] While the canonical tradition in Orthodoxy has a comprehensive compass, Orthodox inter-church instruments have a more limited focus: the constitution of the Standing Conference of Orthodox Bishops in the Americas, for example, deals only with membership, objectives, authority and structure, committees, and meetings.[104] The statute of the Old Catholic Bishops of the Union of Utrecht is similar.[105] A minimalist approach is employed in the constitutions of the Lutheran World Federation,[106] World Alliance of Reformed Churches,[107] and Baptist World Alliance.[108] The subject-matter of the Anglican *ius commune*, on church order, communion relationships, government, ministry, doctrine, liturgy, rites, property, and ecumenism, most resembles the approaches of the Orthodox and Latin churches.

Purpose

Unlike the Anglican *ius commune*, a key function of the instruments of other global ecclesial communities is to organise the global entity institutionally.[109] However, the notion that the Anglican *ius commune* demonstrates and

promotes identity and inter-church unity is commonplace
in the instruments of other global ecclesial communities,
but in different ways. The Old Catholics statute seeks 'to
promote and to realize' communion; it requires the churches, for example, to 'maintain the catholicity, doctrine,
and worship in apostolic succession'.[110] The constitution of
the Standing Conference of Canonical Orthodox Bishops in
the Americas enables the churches through the conference
'to actualize ... unity in all those fields in which a common
effort is required'.[111] One strategic goal of the constitution
of the Lutheran World Federation is to unite the churches,
strengthen them, and help them 'to act jointly in common
tasks'.[112] Similar goals appear in the constitutions of the
World Alliance of Reformed Churches,[113] World Methodist
Council,[114] and Baptist World Alliance.[115] The Latin Code
'facilitates ... an orderly development in the life of both the
ecclesial society and of the individual persons who belong to
it'; laws do not replace faith, grace, and charity[116]; the
supreme law is the salvation of souls.[117] Roman canonists
stress the spiritual, pastoral, educative, protective, unifying,
and ecclesiological purposes of canon law.[118] Similarly, in
the Orthodox tradition, canon law is 'at the service of the
Church ... to guide her members on the way to salvation';
its main function is 'the spiritual growth of the faithful'.[119]

Theological basis
The notion that principles of the Anglican *ius commune*
often articulate theological ideas is also commonplace in the
instruments of other global ecclesial communities. For
Roman Catholic canonists, theology is a direct (material)
source for canon law.[120] Theology concerns judgement
based on knowledge obtained through revelation and canon
law imposes a decision based on that judgement: 'every

single piece of law in the church must be in the service of values either defined or at least controlled by theological reflection'.[121] Others see canon law as *ordinatio fidei*.[122] While some Orthodox separate theology and canon law,[123] in the Lutheran and Reformed tradition, 'the external juridical order of the church should be at the service of the proclamation of the word'; thus, 'the external order must be tested ever anew by the confession of faith, and on no level of legal church life can juridical questions be solved without relation to the church's confession'[124]; church law is not a 'constitutive', but a 'consecutive' and 'regulative' element of a church.[125]

Enforceability

A key difference between the Anglican *ius commune* and instruments of other global ecclesial communities concerns enforceability. Whereas the Anglican entity does not bind internationally but is persuasive, the Latin Code binds all the faithful directly in the particular churches, bishops, clergy, and laity alike.[126] The Eastern Catholic code is similar.[127] In Orthodoxy there is a lively debate as to whether the canonical tradition binds in the sense of letter or spirit.[128] 'Acceptance' of its constitution is required for membership of the Lutheran World Federation.[129] At this point, it is worth noting that the Anglican *ius commune* project is separate from, but related to, the process underway for adoption of an Anglican Covenant. The Lambeth Commission, in its *Windsor Report* (2004), proposed a juridical adoption of a covenant, with each church enacting a brief law, a 'communion law',[130] authorising entry to the covenant.[131] The Covenant Design Group (Nassau, 2007) proposes adoption through formal synodical processes in each church.[132] The Windsor draft covenant itself proposed 'respect' by each church for the principles of canon law common to the churches of the Communion.[133] The Nassau draft covenant proposes that the churches commit themselves to seek a common mind about essential matters 'consistent with ... the canon law of our churches'[134]; the Primates' Meeting 2007 also considered that 'Canon Law should reflect and promote global Communion'.[135]

The Ecumenical Significance of the Anglican *Ius Commune*

Importantly, acknowledgement of an Anglican *ius commune* provides an aid for ecumenical partners seeking a global understanding of Anglicanism, not least those non-Anglican churches which also participate in the canonical tradition.[136] The recognition by Anglican churches of 'the principles of canon law' suggests that canon law itself is perceived as a generic phenomenon, having an existence independent of the legal systems of particular churches and communions. Canon law and its principles overarch individual church legal systems.[137] By way of analogy, canon law may be postulated as an entity in the same way as, in the secular world, civil law or common law. In the secular world, the common law or the civil law are often understood as having an existence independent of the states which operate them. The common law or the civil law is particularised in an individual secular state. As such, people talk of a 'common law system' or a 'civil law system'.[138] Similarly, Anglican legal systems (like Roman Catholic or Orthodox) are 'canon law systems'. Furthermore, the canonical tradition underpinning such systems links churches one to another. These churches live out, in their juridical orders, the canonical tradition. Whether they are conscious of the fact or not, Anglican churches participate in, or belong to, the canon law tradition by perpetuating it through their own legal systems.

In turn, it is possible that the Anglican *ius commune* project might offer a model for the wider ecumenical enterprise itself. Of the member churches of the global ecclesial communities discussed above, each institutional church has its own regulatory system. In the Latin Church, 'particular laws' apply to a specific territory (a particular church,[139] such as a diocese) or a group of people (such as a religious community).[140] Each Eastern Catholic church is *sui juris* (not a concession of the Latin Church) with its own juridical system operative within the common law of the Code of 1990.[141] In Orthodoxy, each local church is either autocephalous (one which elects its own Primate) or autonomous (one which elects its Primate with the participation of the Primate of an autocephalous church), in communion with its sister churches; the Greek Orthodox Archdiocese of America, for example, an eparchy under the canonical jurisdiction of the Ecumenical Patriarchate of Constantinople, is regulated by a Charter, the Holy Scriptures, the Holy Canons, and the regulations promulgated by it; and, as to canonical and ecclesiastical matters not provided therein, by the decisions thereon of the Holy Synod of the Ecumenical Patriarchate.[142] Lutheran churches generally employ constitutions and bylaws: the Lutheran Church of Australia, for example, has a central constitution, bylaws, rules and regulations (which may be amended by its General Synod representative of congregations and pastors), and it recognises custom.[143] In turn, each district of the church, and each congregation within a district, has its own constitution and bylaws which must be consistent with the central constitution and bylaws.[144] By way of contrast, Presbyterian churches employ systems of 'law',[145] or of 'church order'.[146] Other churches employ a plethora of regulatory instruments: in Britain, for example, the Methodist Church has its Constitutional Practice and Discipline expressing 'Methodist Law and Polity'[147]; the United Reformed Church has its Scheme of Union and Manual.[148]

An examination of these laws reveals a wealth of substantive similarities (and not surprisingly differences) between the churches. Some examples may be offered. In *government*, the principle that authority in the church is legislative, executive, and administrative (though churches differ in the distribution of such functions) surfaces in the laws of the Roman Catholic,[149] Old Catholic,[150] Orthodox,[151] Anglican,[152] Lutheran,[153] Presbyterian,[154] and United Reformed churches.[155] In *ministry*, the principle that no minister may be disciplined except by due process (though disciplinary powers are assigned to different institutions) appears in the laws of the Roman Catholic,[156] Old Catholic,[157] Orthodox,[158] Anglican,[159] Lutheran,[160] and Presbyterian churches.[161] In *doctrine*, the principle that the faithful must not publicly dissent from the ecclesiastical doctrine (though laws differ as to which members of the faithful are subject to this) is shared by the Roman Catholic,[162] Orthodox,[163] Anglican,[164] Lutheran,[165] and Presbyterian churches.[166] In *worship*, that the faithful must gather for worship regularly appears in the laws of the Roman Catholic,[167] Anglican,[168] Lutheran,[169] and Presbyterian churches.[170] In relation to *rites*, that baptism (to which rights and duties attach) effects incorporation into the church universal appears in the instruments of the Roman Catholic,[171] Orthodox,[172] Anglican,[173] Lutheran,[174] Presbyterian,[175] and Methodist churches.[176] What the Anglican *ius commune* project shows is that a comparative approach to laws and other regulatory instruments can be deployed imaginatively in ecumenism, through the induction of common principles, to determine in practical ways (despite differences in doctrine) both the scope for and concrete limits on greater visible unity.[177]

Conclusions

This essay is not an exhaustive study of the emergent Anglican *ius commune*. Nor does it provide a theological evaluation of the principles. The *ius commune* idea has emerged at a time of great tension in the world-wide Anglican Communion, and doubtless some may see a causal connection. However, this exercise might have been undertaken, with the same results, at any time. The Anglican *ius commune* concept is not revolutionary. Its articulation merely describes legal facts. Nor is the *ius commune* a binding global legal system imposed by a central Anglican authority. It is not a 'top-down' entity (like the Roman Catholic Code of Canon Law), but a 'grass-roots' development: it emerges organically from the exercise by each church of its own autonomy through its own legal system. The common principles of canon law describe factually what binds Anglicans together in terms of what they share juridically. But it is also more than this. The innovative character of the *ius commune* is that it is an expression for the first time in one document of convergent principles of Anglican canon law, and the numerous benefits of clarity and certainty that flow from that articulation. Moreover, it indicates a collective commitment by the churches of the Communion to a particular way of being part of the church universal. In this respect, it also represents a major resource for ecumenical dialogue, and perhaps even a model for similar projects between ecumenical partners. Finally, as each local church creates for itself its own legal system, as a natural ecclesiastical function, so the *ius commune* may be understood, perhaps especially so in this era of perceived globalisation, as a natural function of the international ecclesial community of the world-wide Anglican Communion. We await with interest discussion of the draft statement of principles of canon law by the Anglican Communion Legal Advisers' Network and its report to the Joint Standing Committee of the Primates' Meeting and the Anglican Consultative Council as the Communion prepares the way for the Lambeth Conference 2008.

Notes

1 Professor Norman Doe is Director of the Centre for Law and Religion, the Law School, Cardiff University. I am extremely grateful to Russell Sandberg, an Associate of the Centre for Law and Religion, Law School, Cardiff University, UK, for his invaluable assistance in preparation of this essay. The essay is based on aspects of N. Doe and R. Sandberg, 'The "state of the union", a canonical perspective: principles of canon law in the Anglican Communion', *Sewanee Theological Review* 49.2 (2006) 234, and a presentation at the Liverpool conference of the Ecclesiastical Law Society 2007.

2 See generally N. Doe, *Canon Law in the Anglican Communion* (Oxford: Clarendon Press, 1998).

3 National, regional, or provincial churches each have their own national law, regional law, or provincial law. These laws are usually located in three distinct sources: a constitution, a code of canons, and a miscellany of other regulatory instruments (such as regulations, rules, decrees, or acts). In addition, many churches have diocesan law, a constitution, and a code of canons.

4 E.g. Scottish Episcopal Church: the code is supplemented by resolutions of its synod.

5 E.g. the Province of Southern Africa has a constitution, a code of canons, and collections of other instruments (such as *acts* of the provincial synod).

6 Wales, Const. I.1.1: the constitution consists *inter alia* of 'all rules and regulations made from time to time by or under the authority or with the consent of the Governing Body'.

7 Australia, Const. XII.74: ' "ordinance" includes any act canon constitution statute legislative measure or provision of a provincial or diocesan synod'.

8 Central Africa, Const., Definitions: 'resolution' is 'any expression of the judgment or opinion of Synod, which is intended to have an appreciative, hortatory or advisory and not a mandatory effect'.

9 Following the general model of the rubrics of the Book of Common Prayer 1662.

10 Canada, Book of Alternative Services (1985): 'For the rest of the service local custom may be established and followed'; Scotland, Can. 1.1: episcopal ordination takes place in accordance with 'the law and custom of the ancient church'; South East Asia, Const, Preamble: that dioceses are associated as a province is 'in accordance with the accepted traditions and usages of the Anglican Communion'.

11 M. Hill, *Ecclesiastical Law* (2nd edn, Oxford: Oxford University Press, 2001) para. 1.32.

12 Australia, Can. 11 1992, 4: this lists canons of 1603 which have 'no operation or effect in a diocese which adopts this canon'; but a diocese may adopt them if it so wishes.

13 England, Submission of the Clergy Act 1533.

14 N. Doe (1998), op. cit., pp. 343ff.

15 See e.g. Lambeth Commission on Communion, *Windsor Report* (2004), p.11.

16 In this essay, the terms 'Anglican common law' or 'Anglican *ius commune*' are used interchangeably as titles of convenience for the phenomenon 'principles of canon law common to the churches of the Anglican Communion'.

17 N. Doe, 'Canon law and communion', *Ecclesiastical Law Journal*
   6 (2002), 241; see also N. Doe, 'The common law of the
   Anglican Communion', *Ecclesiastical Law Journal* 7 (2003), 4;
   these are based on N. Doe (1998), op. cit.

18 See the website of the Consultation: www.acclawnet.co.uk.

19 *Windsor Report* (2004), para. 114.

20 These attracted either unqualified or qualified agreement. The
   one rejected was the principle that no minister should refuse to
   baptise an infant, in spite of the presence of the principle in
   rubrics of the Book of Common Prayer 1662 (which is generally
   normative canonically in member churches).

21 Const. Art. 6.2(1).

22 Can. 50.

23 Can. 32.1.

24 Const. Art. XIX.V.

25 E.g. the Roman Catholic Code of Canon Law 1983, c. 9 and the
   Code of the Eastern Catholic Churches 1990, c. 1501.

26 E.g. Australia, Canon 18, 1992: 'a law ... shall be read as
   including a reference to [*inter alia*] a principle, a practice or a
   tradition of the Church of England'.

27 'Custom is the best interpreter of laws': Roman Catholic Code
   (1983) c. 27.

28 'It is the duty of clergy and people to do their utmost not only to
   avoid occasions of strife but also to seek in penitence and
   brotherly charity to heal such divisions': Church of England:
   Can. A8.

29 R. Dworkin, 'Is law a system of rules?', in R. Dworkin (ed.), *The
   Philosophy of Law* (Oxford: Clarendon Press, 1977), p. 38.

30 The laity 'must strive to live according to Christ's teachings, to
   preach the gospel and to realise God's justice in society': Korea,
   Cans. 42–45.

31 See, e.g., Roman Catholic Code (1983) c. 221.

32 See generally *The Canon Law: Letter and Spirit*, The Canon Law
   Society of Great Britain and Ireland (Dublin: Veritas Publications, 1995), p. 77: the principles of law are those which 'have
   been known to canonical tradition [or] the universal and fundamental principles ... contained in the *Regulae Juris*' which

represent 'the vast treasure house of laws and jurisprudence accumulated by the Church in the course of centuries'.

33 Some churches provide for the continuing authority of pre-Reformation canon law: England, Submission of the Clergy Act 1534; Wales, Const. IX.36; compare Australia, Can. 11 1992, 3(1): 'all canon law of the Church of England made prior to the Canons of 1603 ... shall have no operation or effect in a diocese'; however, 4: this lists the canons of 1603 which have no effect in a diocese but a right is reserved to a diocese to adopt them.

34 Listing attendance at worship among the duties of church membership in, e.g. Southern Africa, Chile, Mexico, England, and Korea is probably based on LC 1948, Res. 37.

35 E.g. the requirement to instruct candidates before confirmation: see Melanesia, Cans. A.3-A-D; Ireland, Const. IX.28(1); see also the 1603 Canons, Can. 61.

36 See N. Doe (1998), op. cit., p. 266.

37 Matt. 18:17; 1 Cor. 5:1-5.

38 Thirty-Nine Articles of Religion, Art. 33.

39 See, for example, Canons Ecclesiastical 1603, Can. 26.

40 Indeed, it is sometimes possible to recast the principle as a more specific *rule*; excommunication provisions could be recast as: if an individual engages in certain proscribed forms of conduct, then that person may be excluded from Holy Communion. See, for example, Wales, Book of Common Prayer 1984: here the provision itself is cast as a rule: 'If they do not heed the warning [of a priest about their conduct], the Priest shall report the matter to the Bishop and proceed as he directs'.

41 E.g. when it was founded in 1920 the Church in Wales adopted an abundance of provisions already found in the laws of the Church of Ireland and the Church of England: see N. Doe, *The Law of the Church in Wales* (Cardiff: University of Wales Press, 2002), Ch. 1.

42 It would be interesting to explore possible parallels with secular customary international law.

43 For the principles to be directly enforceable, each church would have to enact a law along the lines of e.g. Southern Africa, Can.

50: 'It is hereby declared that if any question should arise as to the interpretation of the Canons or Laws of this Church, or of any part thereof, the interpretation shall be governed by the general principles of Canon Law thereto applicable'; see also above notes 21–23.

44 See N. Doe (1998), op. cit., Ch. 2. In the Latin Church, only ordained persons possess the power of governance: Code, c. 129.

45 Constitution (1930), Declaration 11: 'Of the authority of the principles and customs set out in the preceding Declarations'.

46 See Uganda, Const. Art. 3: 'In conformity with established Christian doctrine, the Church of this Province shall proclaim and hold that all people have equal value, rights and dignity in the sight of God, and, while mindful to provide for the special needs of different people committed to its charge, shall not allow discrimination in the membership and government of the Church solely on the grounds of colour, sex, tribe or region'.

47 For developments in Scotland, New Zealand, Australia, and England, see N. Doe (1998), op. cit., pp. 264ff.

48 The idea is an old one for Anglicans: see R. Helmholz, 'Richard Hooker and the European *Ius Commune*', *Ecclesiastical Law Journal* 6 (2001), 4.

49 For the difficulties of induction and the formulation of its general principles see N. Doe (1998), op. cit., pp. 374–375: sometimes there is unanimity, sometimes a majoritarian approach has to be used to induce a principle, sometimes principles are induced from the silence of laws.

50 See also G. Jones, 'Thy Grace Shall Always Prevent ...', in A. Linzey and R. Kirker (eds), *Gays and the Future of Anglicanism: Responses to the Windsor Report* (Winchester: O Books, 2005), 117 at pp. 129–133: while the *ius commune* is not the same thing as a juridic bond ... 'in appearance or intention', it 'arose through the accidents of British colonial history', and if so 'it is very poor theology'; its 'origin and authority ... must have ... theological underpinnings'; either it exists 'accidentally, or it is the necessary expression of a deeper coherence of which the Instruments of Unity are the clearest expressions the

Communion has'; it *'should* be nothing more than the elaboration of the founding principles of Anglicanism's orthodox beliefs', 'the working out of some very elementary obligations that are then placed on member churches because they elect into the Communion': any 'notion that the *ius commune* might flourish in the Communion is naive so long as such individuals continue to pay nothing more than lip service to some of the central beliefs of the apostolic faith'.

51 The draft statement has already been used informally by the Church in Wales in its discussions about the structural reform of the constitution of that church.

52 For the evidence from actual laws, see N. Doe (1998), op. cit., pp. 109f.

53 Ibid., p. 145.

54 Ibid., pp. 120ff.

55 See Book of Common Prayer 1662, The Ordering of Priests: 'Will you reverently obey your Ordinary ... and submitting yourselves to their godly judgments?' This is found in the vast majority of churches; see Australia, Can. 15, 1998: 'An oath or affirmation of canonical obedience shall be taken by a member of the clergy on ... ordination ... first licensing ... consecration as an assistant bishop'.

56 See N. Doe (1998), op. cit., p. 144.

57 See England, Canons Ecclesiastical 1603, Can. 113.

58 For an example of this, see Uganda, Const. Art. 3: 'In conformity with established Christian doctrine, the Church of this Province shall proclaim and hold that all people have equal value, rights and dignity in the sight of God, and, while mindful to provide for the special needs of different people committed to its charge, shall not allow discrimination in the membership and government of the Church solely on the grounds of colour, sex, tribe or region.'

59 See: www.acclawnet.co.uk/docs/2003_nd.pdf.

60 Ibid., Principles, Draft, Definitions.

61 Ibid., Principles 1–8.

62 Ibid., Principles 9–14.

63 Ibid., Principles 15–25.

64 Ibid., Principles 26–46.

65 Ibid., Principles 47–59.

66 Ibid., Principles 60–79.

67 Ibid., Principles 80–92.

68 Ibid., Principles 93–100.

69 The laws of churches do not contain separate treatment of this subject. However, aspects of the principles treated in Part I are scattered throughout the laws of churches. For example, Principle 5.6: 'A voluntary declaration, or other form of assent prescribed by law, to comply with ecclesiastical jurisdiction' commonly appears in the laws of churches: see N. Doe (1998), op. cit., pp. 23f.

70 Legal materials in churches dealing with the Anglican Communion are usually very brief and normally appear in constitutional provisions which treat the identity of the individual church (typically as a member church of the Anglican Communion and the general consequences flowing from this): see N. Doe, 'Canon law and Communion', *Ecclesiastical Law Journal* 6 (2002), 241.

71 See N. Doe (1998), op. cit.

72 See e.g. Southern Africa, Const., Preamble: 'it is expedient that the members of a Church, not by law established, should ... formally set forth the terms of the compact under which it is associated'.

73 See N. Doe (1998), op. cit., Ch. 1.

74 See e.g. Australia, Defence Force Ministry, Canon 1985.

75 Typically, Principles 15 and 20 on legislative competence (normally treated in constitutions).

76 E.g. Principle 69 on the nature of marriage.

77 E.g. Principle 64.6: on baptism and confirmation of mature persons.

78 E.g. Principle 25.6: *nemo iudex in sua causa* (an aspect of judicial impartiality).

79 E.g. Principle 47.2: the duty to proclaim the Gospel.

80 E.g. Principle 60.1: baptism effects incorporation into the church of Christ.

81 E.g. Principle 53: worship as a fundamental action of the church.

82 E.g. Principle 28. For the use of guidance, e.g. in the Church of England see N. Doe, 'Ecclesiastical quasi-legislation', in N. Doe, M. Hill, and R. Ombres (eds), *English Canon Law* (Cardiff: University of Wales Press, 1998), pp. 93–103.

83 Such as the principle of the separation of powers (shared with many secular legal systems): for instance, the law of the Province of the West Indies provides that the Provincial Synod may determine matters 'concerning the common life of the Church ... save and except ... such matters as lie within the jurisdiction of the Ecclesiastical Courts': Const. Arts. 3, 4.

84 E.g. Principle 19.1: jurisdiction may be exercised by groups or individuals.

85 E.g. Principle 83.1: registers of baptisms must be kept.

86 E.g. Principle 36.5: no bishop, priest or deacon coming from another diocese shall minister in the host diocese without the permission of the host diocesan bishop.

87 E.g. Principle 44.6: the faithful should attend public worship regularly.

88 E.g. Principle 11: each church is autonomous.

89 See generally N. Doe, 'Modern church law' in J. Witte and F. S. Alexander (eds), *The Cambridge Companion to Law and Christianity* (Cambridge: Cambridge University Press, forthcoming, 2008).

90 Code, cc. 12, 16, 29.

91 A code is a 'comprehensive and systematic arrangement' of laws: G. Nedungatt (ed.), *A Guide to the Eastern Code* (Rome: Pontificio Istituto Orientale, 2002), p. 49.

92 CCEO, c. 1, 1493; D. Motiuk, 'The code of canons of the Eastern Churches: some ten years later', *Studia Canonica* 36 (2002), 189 at 196.

93 T. Ware, *The Orthodox Church* (London: Penguin Books, 1963, reprinted 1991), p. 15.

94 L. Patsavos, 'The canonical tradition of the Orthodox Church', in F. K. Litsas (ed.), *A Companion to the Greek Orthodox Church*

(New York: Greek Orthodox Archdiocese of North and South America, 1984), p. 145.

95 *The Rudder* (first edition 1800), from the metaphor of the church as a ship: 'the members of the Church [are] guided on their voyage through life by means of the holy canons' (Patsavos).

96 Hereafter SCOBA, Const., Art. II; the churches are: Greek, Antiochian, Serbian, Romanian, Bulgarian, Carpatho Russian, Ukrainian, Albanian.

97 Metropolitan Bartholomaios, 'A common code for the Orthodox churches', *Kanon* I (1973), pp. 45–53.

98 It would be interesting to explore, however, the degree to which each translates the principles of local church polity onto the international ecclesial plane.

99 Const. Arts. I-IV.

100 Const. Art. IV: 'None of these provisions shall limit the autonomy of any member church'.

101 See Constitutional Practice and Discipline of the Methodist Church (Britain), pp. 782–3.

102 Const., Art. II.

103 Liturgical law is located outside the Code: Code, c. 2.

104 The constitution is organised in 7 Articles.

105 It deals with the ecclesiological foundations of the union (e.g. the duties of communion and the right of autonomy) and the international bishops' conference (composition, functions, and discipline). The statute is organised on the basis of Preamble, Order, and Rules.

106 This deals with: doctrinal basis; nature and functions; scope of authority; membership and affiliation; organisation; the assembly; the council; national committees; officers and secretariat; finance; and amendments and bylaws. It has 14 Articles; the bylaws treat equivalent subjects.

107 It covers membership, purposes, general council, executive committee, officers, departments, organisation of areas, and amendments. It has 12 Articles; the bylaws deal with associated subjects.

108 It covers: objective; method of operations; membership of the

Baptist World Congress; General Council; executive committee; officers departments; regional fellowships; amendments (as do its bylaws).

109 See above in the footnotes on subject-matter.
110 B. Order, Art. 1.
111 Preamble, Arts. I and V.1.
112 Arts. I-III,V.
113 Arts. I.3 and III (1–9): they include: to unite the member churches in common service wherever needed and practicable; and to aid member churches which may be weak, oppressed or persecuted; and to contribute to the ecumenical movement.
114 For the Constitution, see Constitutional Practice and Discipline of the Methodist Church (Britain), pp. 782–783.
115 Bylaws of the General Council (2002).
116 *Sacrae Disclipinae Leges*, Apostolic Constitution (25 January 1983), promulgating the Code (1983).
117 Latin Code, c. 1752.
118 J. P. Beal, J. A. Coriden and T. J. Green (eds), *New Commentary on the Code of Canon Law* (New York: Paulist Press, 2000), pp. 1–8.
119 L. Patsavos (1984), op. cit., p. 145.
120 T. Urresti, 'Canon law and theology: two different sciences', *Concilium* 8 (1967), 10.
121 L. Orsy, *Theology and Canon Law* (Collegeville, MN: Liturgical Press, 1992), pp. 137, 165: theology 'contains a body of organised knowledge obtained through revelation and reflection of what was revealed; [canon law] consists of a system of norms of action issued by an ecclesiastical authority'; this study also reviews other schools of thought.
122 E. Corecco, *The Theology of Canon Law* (Pittsburgh: Duquesne University Press, 1992).
123 L. Patsavos (1984), op. cit., p. 145.
124 Statement made at the Barmen Synod 31 May 1934 on the German Evangelical Church: quoted by M. Reuver, *Faith and Law: Juridical Perspectives for the Ecumenical Movement* (Geneva: World Council of Churches, 2000), p. 4.
125 Ibid., p. 3.

Code, c. 1; c. 11: merely ecclesiastical laws bind those baptised

8### A FALLIBLE CHURCH

126 Code, c. 1; c. 11: merely ecclesiastical laws bind those baptised in the Catholic church or received into it; universal laws are binding everywhere on all those for whom they were enacted.
127 CCEO, cc. 1489–1491.
128 J. H. Erickson, *The Challenge of Our Past* (Crestwood, New York: St Valdimir's Seminary Press, 1991), Ch. 1.
129 Const., Art. V.
130 That is a law dealing with ecclesial communion (*ius communionis*).
131 Suggested form of law: 'The Governing Body of the Church in Wales authorises the Archbishop of Wales to enter on behalf of this church the Anglican Covenant and commits the Church in Wales to comply and act in a manner compatible with the Covenant so entered': *Windsor Report* (2004) para. 118, n. 61.
132 Report, Anglican Communion News Service (ACNS) (19-2-2007), para. 8.
133 Ibid., Appendix II, Proposed Anglican Covenant, Art. 17.1.
134 Nassau Draft Covenant, Art. 6.3.
135 Points aired in Discussion of the Draft Text for an Anglican Covenant.
136 The elucidation of common principles has been particularly helpful, for instance, in the work of the Colloquium of Anglican and Roman Catholic Canon Lawyers, established in Rome in 1999.
137 See N. Doe, 'The principles of canon law: a focus of legal unity in Anglican and Roman Catholic relations', *Ecclesiastical Law Journal* 5 (1998), 221.
138 See D. Walker, *Oxford Companion to Law* (Oxford: Oxford University Press, 1980), p. 253, 'Common Law Systems' (e.g. UK, USA).
139 Code, 373; bishops govern dioceses as vicars of Christ not 'as vicars of the Roman Pontiff for they exercise power ... in their own right': *Lumen Gentium*, 27.
140 Code, cc. 13, 20, 23–26: custom is law if it is: approved by the relevant legislator; not contrary to divine law; reasonable; observed by a community capable of receiving a law; observed with the intention of introducing a law; and observed for continuous years.

141 Particular churches include patriarchal churches (c. 25), major archiepiscopal churches (c. 151), and metropolitan churches (c. 155). The episcopal synod of a patriarchal church may legislate for that church: c. 1101.

142 Greek Orthodox Archdiocese of America (hereafter GOAA), Charter (2003), Art. 1.

143 Lutheran Church of Australia (hereafter LCA), Const., Arts. VI–IX; III.(k): one of the objects of LCA is to cultivate uniformity in customs.

144 LCA, Bylaws, Art. IV.1: amendments to a congregation constitution must be approved by the District Church Council; congregation must accept the LCA Confession, constitution and bylaws.

145 J. L. Weatherhead (ed.), *The Constitution and Laws of the Church of Scotland* (Edinburgh: Board of Practice and Procedure, Church of Scotland, 1997).

146 Presbyterian Church in America (hereafter PCA), Book of Church Order (hereafter BCO), I.26: the constitution of the Presbyterian Church in America consists of its doctrinal standards set out in the Westminster Confession of Faith, the Larger and Short Catechisms, and its Book of Church Order. Amendment of the Book of Church Order is effected by the General Assembly with the consent of two-thirds of the Presbyteries; and of the Confession of Faith and Larger and Shorter Catechisms by a three-quarters vote of the General Assembly with the consent of three-quarters of the Presbyteries.

147 Constitutional Practice and Discipline (2002), para. 338.

148 They are accumulated in the URC Manual (2000).

149 Code, c. 135.1: 'The power of governance is distinguished as legislative, executive and judicial'.

150 E.g. Polish National Church (USA), Const., Art. VI.1: 'The authority of this Church is vested in three branches, namely: legislative, executive and judicial'.

151 GOAA, Charter: law-making vests in the eparchial synod (Art. 10); adjudication, in the spiritual courts (Art. 9); the administration of monasteries, in the local hierarch (Art. 21).

152 E.g. Church of England: law-making vests in the General Synod

(Synodical Government Measure 1969); administration of a parish, in the Parochial Church Council (Parochial Church Councils (Powers) Measure 1956); and adjudication, in the courts (Ecclesiastical Jurisdiction Measure 1963).

153 Evangelical Lutheran Church in Canada (hereafter ELCIC), Const.: the Convention is 'the highest legislative authority' (Art. X.1); the episcopal president of the National Church Council is 'the chief executive officer' (Art. XII.5); and judicial functions vest in the Court of Adjudication (Art. XVIII).

154 Legislative, administrative, and judicial functions vest in the court of General Assembly.

155 United Reformed Church (Britain), Manual, B: General Assembly is required to: make regulations; appoint moderators of synods; and 'determine when rights of personal conviction are asserted to the injury of the unity and peace' of the URC.

156 Code, c. 221: the faithful have the right not to be punished except in accord with the norm of law.

157 Polish National Church, Const. XXII.

158 GOAA, Charter, 9: a hierarch who judged a case at first instance cannot hear an appeal.

159 N. Doe (1998), op. cit., pp. 86ff.

160 LCA, Const., X: the judicial system of the church must uphold the 'rules of natural justice'.

161 J. L. Weatherhead (ed.) (1997), op. cit., pp. 42ff.

162 Code, cc. 747–755.

163 Archdiocese of Thyateira and Great Britain, Instructions: Apostasy and Restoration.

164 Church in Wales, Const., XI.18 (clergy and laity are subject to the Disciplinary Tribunal for 'teaching, preaching, publishing or professing doctrine or belief incompatible with that of the Church in Wales'; in the Church of England lay people are not subject to doctrinal discipline in church courts.

165 ELCIC, Approved Model Constitution for Congregations, Art. IV.6–9.

166 PCA, BCO, Preface, II.3; I.1.1.

167 Code, c. 214 (right to worship); c. 920 (the duty to receive holy communion).

168 Church of England, Canon B15: the duty of confirmed persons to receive holy communion.
169 ELCIC, Approved Model Constitution for Congregations, Art. III.a.
170 PCA, BCO, III.47.
171 Code, c. 849.
172 Greek Orthodox Archdiocese of Australia, Handbook, Baptisms.
173 Church of England, Can. B21.
174 Evangelical Lutheran Church in South Africa (Natal-Transvaal), Guidelines, 1.10.
175 PCA, BCO, III.56: baptism is not to be delayed.
176 Constitutional Practice and Discipline of the Methodist Church (Britain), Deed of Union, 6; Standing Orders, 010A.
177 In 1974 the Faith and Order Commission of the World Council of Churches adopted an Outline for the study of 'The Ecumenical Movement and Church Law'; it was not pursued: see M. Reuver, *Faith and Law: Juridical Perspectives for the Ecumenical Movement* (Geneva: World Council of Churches, 2000), p. 5.

7

Mark D. Chapman

Where is it all Going? A Plea for Humility

Learning from Lambeth 1867

The first Lambeth Conference of 1867 lasted three days. A few commentators felt this was strange, given that some bishops had sailed from the other side of the world to take part. *The Times* leader writer, for instance, thought that it was 'incongruous to have dragged a Bishop all the way from Honolulu or New Zealand in order to take a seventy-fifth part in a three days' consultation'.[1] Archbishop Charles Longley of Canterbury approached the Conference with great caution. Given that such a gathering was unprecedented, nobody – least of all the Archbishop – knew quite what to expect (and some, including Archbishop William Thomson of York, even refused to attend since they were unclear what sort of authority such a conference could possibly claim over an established church). However, others had high expectations that the Conference might come to a clear decision about the acceptability of certain beliefs. Some felt the need for a central decision-making authority over the whole of the Communion.

The period leading up to the First Lambeth Conference was marked by a number of theological and legal disputes. In the early 1860s there was a lengthy controversy following the publication in 1860 of the collected work, *Essays and Reviews*, which advocated what would nowadays be regarded as a modest critical approach to Scripture. Notoriously the Master of Balliol College, Benjamin Jowett, had asserted that the Bible should be read 'like any other Book'.[2] Others, like the vicar of the University Church in Oxford, J. W. Burgon, were appalled by such a method: 'The Bible', he wrote, 'is none other than *the voice of Him that sitteth upon the Throne!* Every book of it – every chapter of it – every verse of it – every word of it – every syllable of it – (where are we to stop?) every *letter* of it.'[3] Others, including Edward Bouverie Pusey, leader of the Anglo-Catholic party, agreed. To tamper with biblical inerrancy was to threaten the foundation of the Christian faith.

Far away in South Africa there were similar disturbances. The first Bishop of Natal, John William Colenso, was under suspicion of heterodoxy from the Bishop of Cape Town, Robert Gray. The grounds were that in his commentary on Paul's Epistle to the Romans Colenso had claimed that God's love and mercy were offered to all people, even non-Christians:

Every good thought, which has ever stirred within a heathen's mind, is a token of that work which God's good spirit is working within him, as one of the great human family, redeemed by the Love of God in Christ Jesus, and related all to the Second Adam by a second spiritual birth, (of which Baptism is the express sign and seal to the Christian).[4]

If that was not enough to upset the apple cart, Colenso also maintained a relatively tolerant attitude towards polygamous converts.[5] In the 1860s he continued his academic researches, publishing the first volume of his *magnum opus* on the Pentateuch, where he questioned both the numerical accuracy – he had been trained as a mathematician – and the morality of the biblical accounts of the patriarchs.[6] Having alienated both his dean and archdeacon in Pietermaritzburg, Colenso was deposed by Bishop Gray, who had been appointed Metropolitan of Cape Town in December 1853 (shortly after Colenso's consecration), and who claimed metropolitical powers. The long court case, which centred on whether Gray actually held these powers, provoked a crisis between the Church of England and the new overseas Provinces. To consecrate a new bishop for Natal would be tantamount to recognising the deposition of Colenso.

Gray naturally spent some time agitating among his fellow colonial bishops for some sort of declaration that Colenso's views could find no place in the Anglican Communion. Nevertheless, Archbishop Longley was clear that a definitive settlement of the Colenso issue would be to overstep the authority of the Conference. He consequently refused to put a resolution approving the excommunication and deposition of Colenso onto the agenda. This incensed many bishops, which meant that during the debate itself strong resolutions opposing Colenso were brought forward. These were discussed at length by both sides, even though Colenso had very few supporters beyond the redoubtable Connop Thirlwall. Under the influence of the American bishops, what eventually emerged was a statement 'that this conference accepts and adopts the wise decision of the convocation of Canterbury as to the appointment of another bishop to Natal'. This satisfied neither side since there was no condemnation of Colenso's opinions. Consequently, as the bishops were leaving after the Conference Gray organised a stronger petition, which was signed by about two-thirds of the bishops, which declared their 'acceptance of the sentence pronounced upon Dr Colenso by the metropolitan of South Africa, with his suffragans, as being spiritually a valid sentence'. But formally at least the bishops did not definitively rule on the Colenso case – spiritual authority was very different from legal authority, which still rested with the Privy Council. What was most important is that the Conference did not make a hard and fast decision, which would have had the effect of dividing the Communion. For this reason, according to Alan Stephenson (somewhat overstating the case), Longley 'deserves an important place among the heroes of Anglicanism'.[7] In terms of the future development of the Anglican Communion, what is central is that a degree of comprehension survived, despite the hostility to Colenso.

The importance of refraining from controversy was noted by William Ewart Gladstone, who soon afterwards was to become Prime Minister. Shortly before the Lambeth Conference he wrote to his friend, Alexander Penryn Forbes, Bishop of Brechin in the Scottish Episcopal Church, that he could not

> ... but regard with interest and with anxiety the approaching assemblage at Lambeth. I can conceive its doing great good. I most earnestly hope it will avoid polemics, and will condemn no persons or bodies either on the Protestant, the Roman or the Eastern side. There is something in all, it seems to me, that is to be cherished, though of course with great differences in the three cases.

In what I have said I do not mean to imply that Bishop Gray should not be supported: but I trust it will not be upon narrow grounds.[8]

Gladstone hoped that the Conference might assist the reunion of the scattered Christian churches, and act as a witness to other denominations of the unity of the Anglican Communion. At a time when the Roman Catholic Church was beginning to move towards holding its own general council, the Lambeth Conference might have functioned as a forum to show the catholicity of the Anglican churches, which might even have led the Pope to invite their bishops. What was therefore crucial was that the Conference steered clear of polemics.

Forbes, however, who was a close friend of Dr Pusey, although sharing Gladstone's hopes for reunion, felt that the Conference should deliberately distance the Anglican churches from the Reformation and offer a decisive doctrinal statement. Some Anglican bishops, led by Henry John Whitehouse of Illinois, who preached the opening sermon at the Conference, had expressed a hope that the Swedish bishops might be invited. This provoked an outcry from Pusey who doubted Scandinavian orthodoxy on account of their adherence to Lutheran doctrine. Forbes went even further than his mentor. In a letter to the church newspaper, the *Guardian*, he pointed to the prevalence of illegitimate births in Sweden as evidence of the weakness of Christianity in that country. Later, he even went as far as saying that the Prayer Book injunction to avoid heresy would be difficult in Stockholm with its high number of 'fornicators'.[9] Forbes, together with other Anglo-Catholic bishops, was keen on promoting a firm moral and doctrinal lead from the first assembly of Anglican bishops. In this way it would function as a kind of general council. For Forbes, the Lambeth Conference would become the natural successor to the old political establishment. This appeared to be dying even in England and was long since buried elsewhere, including in his native Scotland. A general council, he held, would act as a safeguard against the present condition of Anglicanism, which was 'not only essentially provisional, but universally perilous'.[10] Although Forbes was prevented from attending the Conference through illness, his views are representative of those for whom an assembly of bishops would function as a supreme authority over the world-wide church.

There are obvious parallels between the First Lambeth Conference and recent developments in Anglicanism. Indeed, disagreements over the purpose and authority of the First Lambeth Conference reveal that calls for definitive rulings, decisive moral leadership, and a lack of provisionality in Anglicanism are certainly nothing new. The idea of Anglicanism as a balance between those who disagreed with one another was not considered a virtue by many bishops in 1867. Nevertheless, through skilful (or possibly incompetent) chairmanship Longley ensured that breadth was maintained. The way in which the provinces had developed, even by 1867, gave effective control to the national churches rather than to the Archbishop of Canterbury, something that was particularly obvious in the American and Scottish churches, which were totally free from the influence of the British Crown. This meant that there could be no agreed mechanism to solve disputes, since canons could not transcend national boundaries. Consequently, while resolutions could be adopted by Lambeth Conferences, there was no central power to put them into practice. Again the Colenso case is illuminating. Even though a new bishop for Natal was consecrated, Colenso remained in place thanks to the ruling of the Privy Council, and a parallel jurisdiction developed.

There are evidently many voices across the contemporary Anglican world who would urge the Communion to develop some sort of decisive teaching authority – and the recent efforts towards the formulation of an Anglican Covenant are moving cautiously in that direction. It is too early to know whether it will be an effective mechanism for solving disputes, although it is interesting that in the draft there is a recognition that the Anglican Instruments of Communion have no canonical status in the different Provinces.[11] What seems doubtful is that many Provinces will accord such a high degree of decision-making authority to the Primates as that proposed in the draft. Since I have discussed these developments in detail elsewhere,[12] however, in the remainder of this chapter I want to explore some of the more general issues emerging from the first Lambeth Conference which relate to the nature of Anglicanism (and to the Church more broadly).

Openness and Closure

Many of the bishops in 1867 sought a closure to the Colenso crisis: as Forbes noted, 'provisionality' was not considered appropriate for a church which claimed to possess the truth, and it could look weak and indecisive to those outside. This was particularly true of a weak, state-controlled church like the Church of England which was far too broad and inclusive to be able to resist what Forbes called 'the advancing and all devouring Rationalism of the xix century'.[13] Instead what seemed to be required was an independent form of ecclesiastical sovereignty exercised by the bishops in council, as inheritors of the authority of the apostles themselves. While many churches adopted synodical structures, sometimes with significant lay participation (as in the USA), what was important was that the church had to possess its own source of authority if it was to withstand the assaults of an increasingly infidel state. In passing, it need hardly be said that there are obvious similarities between this sort of outcry against rationalism and some of the recent attacks that have been made against what is perceived to be the inexorable march of secular liberalism, particularly in the American church (by, for example, Ephraim Radner and Philip Turner).[14]

In response to what they regarded as a crisis of authority, there was, both for Forbes and Pusey, a need to locate the source of authority in something definitive and fixed in order to guard against the dangers of liberalism. Chipping away at the edifice of faith could lead to a disastrous collapse. As Henry Liddon put it in his biography of Pusey: the proverb 'nemo repente turpissimus [No man becomes a villain all at once] finds its analogy in the progress of theoretic unbelief'. Citing Pusey, he continued,

This is a characteristic of all who have parted with faith, that they began with some one point. They parted, as they thought, with one point of Faith; the event showed that they parted with the Faith itself ... The form of heresy was different; the principle was the same. Man trusted his own conceptions of what a Revelation from God should be, what it were fitting for the Infinite God to do and be, rather than submit blindly to what God had revealed of Himself, that, not trusting in his own light, he might receive, pure and unmixed, the light from God. [Men] make their own notions the criterion of the Mind of God; not the revealed Mind of God the corrective of their own thoughts.[15]

Faith, then, involved self-surrender to the supernaturally revealed truth. This meant that there could be no space for the sort of unbelief demonstrated by Colenso. As Pusey wrote to his friend and fellow Tractarian, John Keble:

> It is the old story, 'who is to bell the cat?' Here, in Oxford, we seem to be so familiar with our evils as to acquiesce in them, sleeping in the snow, which is death ... And now Bp. Colenso is striving to make a position in the Church for his unbelief. And then the Church would be (God forbid) dead. I used to maintain and do maintain, that the Church must bear with much, for fear of worse evils. But she must not bear with this naked denial of our Lord the Atoner, and of God the Holy Ghost Who spake by the Prophets ... I never felt so desponding as I do now, not at people's attacks (these we must expect) but at the acquiescence in them on the part of religious men.[16]

For many Anglo-Catholics, including Pusey, there was a need to submit to a revelation which was to be found primarily in what I have called a 'catholicism of the Word',[17] which identified the teaching of the catholic church (and consequently the Church of England) with the teachings of the undivided church of the first five centuries or so. Such teaching was interpreted by the successors to the apostles, the bishops, which meant that truth was clear and unambiguous.

Nowadays there are few Puseyites left in the Anglican Communion. However, there are many who use similar arguments, but who represent other traditions. Most recently, for instance, Henry Luke Orombi, the outspoken Archbishop of Uganda, has focused on the Word of Scripture as interpreted according to the Reformation formularies in his definition of authentic Anglicanism: 'The basis of our commitment to Anglicanism is that it provides a wider forum for holding each other accountable to Scripture, which is the seed of faith and the foundation of the Church in Uganda.' He goes on: 'For the Ugandan church to compromise God's call of obedience to the Scriptures would be the undoing of more than 125 years of Christianity through which African life and society have been transformed.' Again there is a sense that there can be no halfway house or compromises. Indeed, with reference to the contemporary problems being experienced in Anglicanism he boldly asserts:

We would not be facing the crisis in the Anglican Communion if we had upheld the basic Reformation convictions about Holy Scripture: its primacy, clarity, sufficiency, and unity. Part of the genius of the Reformation was its insistence that the Word of God and the liturgy be in the language of the people – that the Bible could be read and understood by the simplest plowboy. The insistence from some Anglican circles (mostly in the Western world) on esoteric interpretations of Scripture borders on incipient Gnosticism that has no place in historic or global Anglicanism.

The ultimate authority in Anglicanism rests in Scripture, interpreted as the 'power of the Word of God precisely as the *Word* of God – written to bring transformation in our lives, our families, our communities, and our culture'.[18]

Although Pusey's 'catholicism of the Word' is replaced by Scripture as the single authority, the effect is much the same: any challenge to scriptural supremacy is understood as an assault on the very substance of the Christian faith itself. No doubt the divisions over biblical interpretation derive in part from a range of post-colonial problems, including the 'coming of age' of the massive African churches and what Orombi called the end of the 'long season of British hegemony'. These have only recently begun to be seriously investigated.[19] There is an obvious power struggle going on both between the global south and north, as well as between conservatives and liberals within many of the 'northern' churches, some of which masquerades as questions of biblical interpretation (about which much could be written).[20] However, what I want to focus on is the idea of a clearly identifiable truth as resting at the heart of Anglicanism.

As both of these examples show, the notion of Anglicanism as resting on a fixed and easily demonstrable truth challenges Anglican comprehensiveness. Comprehensiveness has perhaps been the most popular model of Anglicanism which sees it as embracing a number of co-existing church parties, each understanding Christianity in its own way, but all at home within one and the same church. A singular fixed theological system based on one particular version of truth will mean that those adopting different theological methods will inevitably be unchurched. As Orombi suggested, certain varieties of biblical interpretation can be labelled 'Gnosticism' (although he does not say what he means by the term), which means that they are heretical and thus have no place in Anglicanism. Pusey and Newman were similarly willing to label liberalism and rationalism as heresies and thus as not deserving a place within the Anglican fold.

Other figures from a more moderate theological background have been equally critical of what they regard as the
weakness of Anglican comprehensiveness, even though they
have been less willing to label opponents as heretics. Stephen Sykes, for instance, at the time Professor in Durham,
offered a powerful critique of what he regarded as the disastrous theology of comprehensiveness. He wrote in
response to the theological controversies of the 1970s which
culminated in the failure of the Church of England Doctrine Commission to come to an agreement about what it
believed, which led to the contested report *Christian
Believing*[21]:

> Coined at a time when internal party strife was at its most
> acute, [comprehensiveness] apparently offered a non-
> partisan refuge for that large body of central Anglicans
> who properly speaking belonged to no party ... Theo-
> logically speaking, however, the effect of the proposal has
> been disastrous. It must be stated bluntly that it has
> served as an open invitation to intellectual laziness and
> self-deception. Maurice's opposition to system-building
> has proved a marvellous excuse to those who believe they
> can afford to be condescending about the outstanding
> theological contribution of theologians from other com-
> munions and smugly tolerant of second-rate theological
> competence of their own; and the failure to be frank
> about the issues between the parties in the Church of
> England has led to an ultimately illusory self-projection
> as a Church without any specific doctrinal or confessional
> standpoint.[22]

Sykes' critique of 'comprehensiveness' was aimed against
what he regarded as the vague talk of 'complementarity',

whereby a blend of different truths could be held together
in diversity. He traced the origin of this understanding to
the 'conflict between evangelical and anglo-catholic in the
nineteenth century ... It was a theory with an irresistible
attraction for bishops endeavouring to achieve a *modus
vivendi* between warring groups in their dioceses.'[23]
Nevertheless, Sykes regarded complementarity as little
more than muddled thinking: 'Lots of contradictory things
may be said to be complementary by those with a vested
interest in refusing to think straight.'[24] Against what he
regarded as such loose thinking, Sykes challenged those
who would defend diversity to justify themselves theologically.[25] He developed his own solution to what he regarded
as the lack of Anglican rigour on the basis of common
liturgy and practice (which could lead to a frightening
vision of a church controlled by the Liturgical Commission).[26] While few would want to counsel the Anglican
Communion to adopt muddled thinking, there still seems
to me to be something important – and theologically
defensible – in the notion of comprehensiveness.

Against Systems

Rather surprisingly, given their almost saint-like status,
Sykes reserves particular venom for F. D. Maurice, one of
the most important theologians of the Victorian period, and
Michael Ramsey, Archbishop of Canterbury through the
1960s, who had been deeply influenced by Maurice. Both
are accused (correctly) of resisting systems, and by impli-
cation of a lack of coherent theological thinking. Yet to
some extent Sykes misses the point. Indeed a theological
justification of diversity might even be founded on their
theologies. Maurice resisted systems precisely because he

saw them as reducing Christianity to a controllable and bounded system which focused in on itself, rather than pointing beyond itself to God, who simply could not be contained by any system. Maurice was not a theorist of complementarity, but upheld a deeper truth which he identified with the Catholic Church which could be possessed by no group or party ('system') within the church. The different systems in the church, the 'Protestant, Romish, English,' he wrote, 'seem to me to bear witness of a *Divine Order*; each to be a miserable, partial, human substitute for it'.[27] Truth was not a blend of competitors, but a goal or a quest to which all aspired:

> Our church has no right to call herself better than other churches in any respect, in many she must acknowledge herself to be worse. But our position, we may fairly affirm, for it is not a boast but a confession, is one of singular advantage ... [O]ur faith is not formed by a union of Protestant systems with the Romish system, nor of certain elements taken from the one and of certain elements taken from the others. So far as it is represented in our liturgy and our articles, it is the faith of a church and has nothing to do with any system at all. That peculiar character which God has given us, enables us, if we do not slight the mercy, to understand the difference between a Church and a System.[28]

Although the man who refuses to belong to a party or a system in the church might be accused of 'Eclecticism or Syncretism' (or even comprehensiveness, although Maurice does not use the term), he 'will understand he who endeavours to substitute a Church for systems, must regard with most dread and suspicion the attempt at a complete, all-comprehending system'.[29] The Catholic Church was bigger than any one expression. Indeed, the Church did not 'comprehend' all existing systems, but instead criticised them all.

Similarly, writing nearly a century later, Michael Ramsey was aware of the ambiguous nature of truth in the church. 'The Church', he wrote, 'is a scene of continual dying; yet it is the place where the sovereignty of God is known and uttered, and where God is reconciling the world to Himself.'[30] For Ramsey, life in the Church is a recognition both of the triumph and glory of the Church, but also of the provisionality and partiality of all concrete expressions of Christianity. Within any church there was always the need to be aware of the temptation to make one's own partial truth into a system. The Church was thus to bear witness, not to the perfection of those who share in it,

> but to the Gospel of God by which alone, in which alone, in one universal family, mankind can be made perfect. It is not something Roman or Greek or Anglican; rather does it declare to men their utter dependence upon Christ by setting forth the universal Church in which all that is Anglican or Roman or Greek or partial or local in any way must share in an agonizing death to its pride.[31]

The Gospel guarded against the temptation towards idolatry by forcing upon us a dying to self through the repeated rehearsal of the drama of the death and resurrection of Christ. Although this process could never be complete, it nevertheless served to deliver us 'from partial rationalisms', into an

> orthodoxy which no individual and no group can possess ... As he receives the Catholic Sacrament and recites the

Catholic creed, the Christian is learning that no single movement nor partial experience within Christendom can claim his final obedience, and that a local Church can claim his loyalty only by leading him beyond itself to the universal family which it represents.[32]

The same themes can be detected in Rowan Williams' writings. Like Maurice and Ramsey, he too is resistant to the enticements of systems, and is deeply aware of the need for a careful critique of the ways in which power is expressed within all groups in the Church. The task of theology, he once wrote, is to disclose 'the kind of ideological bondage that threatens to take over a Church-based or a Church-focused theology'.[33] In an early programmatic essay he wrote of the need to expose the 'destructive longing for final clarity, totality of vision, which brings forth the monsters of religious and political idolatry'.[34] What he termed Catholic Orthodoxy presents 'a challenge to the shrinking of a tradition to the dimension of one person's or one group's need, for comfort and control'.[35] On such a model there could be no simple clarity and no straightforward system: 'To be introduced into relation with [Jesus Christ],' Williams wrote, 'is to encounter what is not exhaustible in word or system ... it is to step into faith (rather than definitive enlightenment).' Faith rests not so much in a submission to a system, whatever one's intellectual reservations (which is the pattern of faith espoused by Pusey), but far more on the acceptance of 'the questioning story of a crucified and resurrected Lord' which disturbs all securities. This makes faith less reliant on revelation and far more on a relationship with Jesus Christ, who always lies beyond the control of any system.[36]

Conclusion

This survey of anti-systematic thought is obviously far from
exhaustive, but it does at least clarify one of the most serious and divisive problems of contemporary Anglicanism.
Longley's handling of the 1867 Lambeth Conference
offered a solution to Anglican disputes that was hardly
likely to meet with much agreement from those who sought
to create clear boundaries to the dogmatic and moral
theology of the Anglican Communion. Those whose
theologies rested on systems were dissatisfied with the
solution. The same holds true today – those with clear
systems are likely to make accusations of heresy against
those with whom they disagree, and may well try to expel
them from the Communion altogether. And it is important
to note, with Maurice, that this is equally as true for 'liberals' as for the catholics and evangelicals I have used as
examples.[37] However, against such systems there is an
alternative type of theology. Its starting point, at least on the
model adopted by Maurice and Ramsey and Williams, is
that we may well be wrong, and we ought at least to expose
ourselves to the possibility that we are. We ought to listen
and to learn, but also to resist those who feel that their way
is the only way. One of the joys of Anglicanism is that it is
limited to particular national or provincial churches with
their diverse cultures and contexts – none of which, however globalised, can ever be universal. Whether structures
can be created that will promote such listening to those
from other contexts is an open question. But nothing will
happen unless there is a recognition of frailty, fallibility, and
humility by all those involved in the Windsor process. Such
vulnerability may not be fashionable, but a refusal to lord it
over others even to the point of death is not without an

important theological precedent. This need for humility and vulnerability does not seem too far removed from some words from Rowan Williams written nearly twenty years ago, which in hindsight seem decidedly prescient:

[T]he notion of a Church whose unity lies primarily, if not absolutely and simply, in a shared attention to, and an attention to how [the questioning story of a crucified and resurrected Lord] is being assimilated in diverse and distant communities, culturally and historically strange, is not without relevance in our own day.[38]

Notes

1 *The Times*, 14 September 1867, p. 8.
2 *Essays and Reviews* (London: Longmans, tenth edn, 1862), p. 455.
3 J. W. Burgon, *Inspiration and Interpretation* (Oxford: Parker, 1861), p. 89.
4 J. W. Colenso, *The Epistle of St. Paul to the Romans. Newly translated and explained from a Missionary Point of View* (London: Macmillan, 1863); new edition edited by Jonathan A. Draper: *Commentary on Romans* (Pietermaritzburg: Cluster Publications, 2003), p. 107.
5 *A Letter to the Archbishop of Canterbury. Upon the Proper Treatment of Polygamist Converts from Heathenism* (London: Macmillan, 1862).
6 J. W. Colenso, *The Pentateuch and the Book of Joshua Critically Examined* (London: Longmans, 1862).
7 See Alan Stephenson, *The First Lambeth Conference, 1867* (London: SPCK, 1967), ch. 11.
8 Gladstone to Forbes, 17 August 1867, cited in *Alexander Penrose Forbes: Bishop of Brechin, the Scottish Pusey* (London: SPCK, 1939), p. 135.

9 *Guardian*, 28 August 1867, p. 933; 11 Sept 1867, p. 971.

10 Forbes to Gladstone, 15 August 1867, cited in Rowan Strong, *Alexander Forbes of Brechin: The First Tractarian Bishop* (Oxford: Clarendon Press, 1995), p. 202.

11 Anglican Communion Office, *An Anglican Covenant: A Draft for Discussion* (April 2007), §6. This document is available at: www.anglicancommunion.org/commission/d_covenant/docs/ Draft%20Covenant%20Text%2020070504.pdf.

12 See my introduction and chapter in Mark D. Chapman (ed.), *The Anglican Covenant: Unity and Diversity in the Anglican Communion* (London: Continuum, 2007).

13 Letter of Forbes to Victor de Buck, 20 February 1870, in Forbes Correspondence, Pusey House Library, Oxford.

14 Ephraim Radner and Philip Turner, *The Fate of Communion: The Agony of Anglicanism and the Future of a Global Church* (Grand Rapids: Eerdmans, 2006), pp. 20–21.

15 H. P. Liddon, *Life of Pusey* (second edn, London: Longmans, 1897), 4 vols, iv, p. 8.

16 Pusey to Keble, 6 November 1862, cited in Liddon, *Life of Pusey*, iv, p. 24.

17 'A Catholicism of the Word and a Catholicism of Devotion: Pusey, Newman and the first *Eirenicon*' in *Journal for the History of Modern Theology* (forthcoming, 2007).

18 Henry Luke Orombi, 'What is Anglicanism?' in *First Things* (August/September 2007) at: http://firstthings.com/article.php3? id_article=6002.

19 See my *Anglicanism: A Very Short Introduction* (Oxford: Oxford University Press, 2006), ch. 1; Ian T. Douglas and Kwok Pui-Lan (eds), *Beyond Colonial Anglicanism* (New York: Church Publishing Inc., 2001); and Kevin Ward, *A History of Global Anglicanism* (Cambridge: Cambridge University Press, 2006), ch. 15.

20 Miranda K. Hassett, *Anglican Communion in Crisis: How Episcopal Dissidents and Their African Allies are Reshaping Anglicanism* (Princeton: Princeton University Press, 2007).

21 Doctrine Commission of the Church of England, *Christian Believing: The Nature of the Christian Faith and its Expression in Holy Scripture and Creeds* (London: SPCK, 1976).

22 Stephen Sykes, *The Integrity of Anglicanism* (Oxford: Mowbray, 1978), p. 19.

23 Ibid., p. 34.

24 Ibid., p. 19.

25 Ibid., pp. 6–7.

26 See Richard Roberts, 'Lord, Bondsman and Church' in Colin Gunton and Daniel Hardy, *On Being the Church* (Edinburgh: T & T Clark, 1989), pp. 156–224.

27 F. D. Maurice, *The Kingdom of Christ or Hints on the Principles, Ordinances and Constitution of the Catholic Church in letters to a Member of the Society of Friends* (reprint of second edn, London: James Clarke, 1959), 2 vols, ii, p. 314.

28 Ibid., p. 329.

29 Ibid., p. 316.

30 A. Michael Ramsey, *The Gospel and the Catholic Church* (London: Longmans, Green and Co., 1936), p. 41.

31 Ibid., p. 66.

32 Ibid., p.135.

33 Rowan Williams, 'Theology and the Churches' in Robin Gill and Lorna Kendall (eds), *Michael Ramsey as Theologian* (London: DLT, 1995), pp. 9–28, p. 22.

34 'What is Catholic Orthodoxy?' in R. D. Williams and Kenneth Leech (eds), *Essays Catholic and Radical* (London: Bowardean Press, 1983), pp. 11–25, p. 25.

35 Ibid., p. 18.

36 'Does it make sense to speak of a pre-Nicene Orthodoxy?' in Rowan Williams (ed.), *The Making of Orthodoxy* (Cambridge: Cambridge University Press, 1989), pp. 1–23, pp. 17–18.

37 Maurice, op.cit., p. 308.

38 'Does it make sense to speak of a pre-Nicene Orthodoxy?', p. 18.

8

Kenneth Stevenson

Communion and Conflict

Stories

Communion and conflict is an experience I first encountered in childhood. I was brought up in the Scottish Episcopal Church, and when we switched from travelling from
one church to attending another, I was immediately aware
of a shift into a slightly different tradition. It wasn't to do
with what is sometimes called 'churchmanship'. It was
more to do with background and religious culture. For the
Episcopal Church has long had within its bounds two
contrasting strands. One is English-based, perhaps more
liberal in theology, preferring the English liturgy, whereas
the other is the milieu of a more native-based church
culture, often more conservative in theology, and more
influenced by the Oxford Movement, with an historic pre-
ference for the Scots liturgy. Obviously the two have over-
lapped and still overlap, and could coexist in the same
congregation.

Then, on one of my first visits to St Mary's Cathedral,
Edinburgh, I was shown a painting of the consecration of
Samuel Seabury as the first bishop of the Episcopal Church
of the USA in 1784. Because he was refused consecration in

England, he had to travel north to receive it from an independent Church that owed no allegiance to King George III. One of the byproducts of this event was the export of parts of the Scots liturgy across the Atlantic Ocean, with consequences that persist to this day, instanced in the explicitly consecratory role given to the Holy Spirit in the celebration of the Eucharist – an important legacy now common coin in many parts of the Anglican Communion.

As time went on, I became increasingly aware of other diversities. The village in which we lived had two Church of Scotland parishes. The Old Kirk had always been Church of Scotland, and the common cup had always been used at Communion. The other parish had belonged to the United Free Church of Scotland, and although the two had joined together in 1929, the old UF tradition was more evangelical in its theology, and the individual cup was used at Communion. When the two parishes were eventually joined, and shared the same service, as at Christmas, one side would receive from the common cup, whereas the other would use individual cups – which led to some smart rearrangements in the seating of the congregation as the pre-communion hymn proceeded.

Pressure to share communion across the denominational divides reared its head on special occasions, and it was usually at festivals, when the Presbyterian spouse often wanted to communicate with the Episcopalian partner. Here practice varied, and one sensed a paradoxical result, namely that clergy trained in the 'English', more liberal school were more welcoming than those from the stricter 'Scottish' tradition: some of them were more sensitive to the need for separate identity, fed on historic rivalries that go back to the eighteenth century, when the Episcopal

Church was decimated by persecution as a result of its support for the Jacobite cause, after the Hanoverian succession. In time these attitudes softened considerably (I am speaking of the 1950s), and there was already pressure for intercommunion in educational institutions. As a student at Edinburgh University in the late 1960s, I experienced how the chaplaincies had to come to terms with this factor, between Presbyterians, Anglicans, and Methodists, and I found myself as a member of the Scottish Episcopal Church's Commission on Inter-Communion.[1] It was an interesting challenge to thrash out some kind of policy on a matter which at the time was both controversial and for some quite painful. From the very beginning of our deliberations, we found ourselves faced with three different approaches, which offered differing solutions. In the jargon of the time, they were called Views A, B, and C.

View A was the traditional Catholic and Orthodox approach, which regarded communion as the sign of an already-existing unity. It was, on this showing, impossible for Christians to share the Lord's Supper together unless and until there was agreement in doctrine and order about what the Eucharist and the Church were meant to be.

View B was the traditional Evangelical approach, which regarded communion as a sign of fellowship between believers. Confirmation, an important 'marker' for some, was taken to be Anglicanism's internal discipline, which should not be allowed to 'unchurch' or denigrate other Christian communities.

More recently, a third approach had come forward (View C), to which most of us on the Commission tilted. This was about Christians working together, in worship and witness in a committed relationship. In such contexts, the Church is neither monolithic, nor a loose federation of the likeminded. Communion takes seriously the relationship between the Church as given and the Church in its coming fullness.

Many of the differences I observed in childhood have either disappeared (the Scottish Episcopal Church has become more consciously 'Scottish' over the years) or they have recreated themselves in new ways (the two traditions of the churches in our old village may be long forgotten, but there are growing tensions in the Kirk between conservative evangelicals and others). As Anglicans, we are now far more generous about inter-communion than we were at that time. And yet, while there is a difference between sharing communion together and being 'in communion' with each other as a result of ecumenical agreement, I keep coming back to those three approaches, those three 'Views' – especially when I contemplate today's more widely publicised divisions, and see the results of 'View C' in such ecumenical miracles as the Porvoo Agreement of Anglicans and Lutherans in Northern Europe. But before I return to this question, I want to make one further point of comparison.

Whereas these experiences were largely about separated Christians striving to be able to share communion with each other, around the time of my consecration as a bishop in the Church of England (1995) this coincided with the tensions accruing from the recent Episcopal Ministry Act of Synod (1994) for those opposed to the ordination of women. Under these provisions, those parishes unable to accept a bishop who ordained women could request what is called 'extended Episcopal ministry'. The use of the term 'impaired communion' entered the collective language of the Church of England at this time, under which some clergy (and their Provincial Episcopal Visitors – often referred to as 'flying bishops') abstained from receiving communion, particularly from women-ordaining bishops. We thus have entered another scenario altogether. We are no longer talking about separated Christians finding ways of sharing the Eucharist together, but parts of the same Church refusing to share communion because of a supposed ecclesiological rupture in relationships. For me, the irony of the situation was expressed at my consecration, where two robed Roman Catholic priests received communion – whereas the flying bishop, had he been there, would not.

I am not alone in struggling hard with the notion of 'impaired communion', a term mentioned – but recognised for its inadequacy – at the Lambeth Conference in 1988. I do not want to appear to be going to the opposite extreme, of 'whipping people in' to receive communion together. But communion is a gift, not a weapon. The bottom line for me (and I suspect for many others) is that we are either in communion or we are not – and there can be no halfway house. That is a challenge that faces those working hard to make some kind of provision for those opposed to women bishops, without conceding what is to all intents and purposes a separate church but pretends not to be, which would be an ecclesiological nonsense. It is not possible to have the Church on one's own terms, otherwise we run the risk of turning it into some kind of religious supermarket, where you take what you want, refuse what you don't want, and complain when something is not available! There seems to be something singularly unattractive about parts of Western culture that motivate us to opt out of difficult situations, instead of taking up the challenge and actually working away at those disagreements. It is as if we are reliving those three 'Views' of inter-communion on the

grand scale, either with everything sorted out first (invariably argued strenuously – but unconvincingly – by the
Vatican), or not being fussy about ecclesiological details but
including all who love the Lord in a particular (evangelical)
way, or else holding to an eschatological perspective that is
more trusting, and more costly. It may be appropriate at
this point, therefore, to look at the background to that
crucial word, 'communion'.

Communion in History

In 1996, Nicholas Sagovsky delivered the Hulsean Lectures
in Cambridge, which were subsequently written up into an
important (and undervalued) little book, entitled *Ecumenism, Christian Origins and the Practice of Communion.*[2] It is
one of those rare publications that combine good historical
scholarship with an awareness of the Church's position
today. (The only drawback is the price – perhaps a casualty
of the publisher's decision to produce it in hardback only!)
The trouble with 'Communion' is that it is a slippery word,
part of ecumenical-speak. But Sagovsky sets it in a far wider
perspective, placing it originally in the world of Greek
philosophy, and of fruitful civic relationships in the ancient
world, with all the tensions that this implies, whether about
leadership (Plato's philosopher-king) or dissent (Socrates
was too hot to handle and had therefore to be done away
with). And while there was no exact equivalent in Israel,
Sagovsky shows lines of comparison between 'communion'
and 'covenant' – that binding relationship between the
people, their God, and one another.

Given the Greek background alongside which the early
Church developed, it was almost inevitable that 'communion' should figure in the vocabulary of Christianity and the

grammar of its lifestyle, to which the New Testament bears witness. In the later fourth century, Basil of Caesarea, Gregory of Nazianzus, and Gregory of Nyssa develop 'communion' in terms of relations within the Trinity as well as our knowledge of God in the Christian community. And Augustine is responsible for the evolution of this transition into Latin through the use of such terms as 'communio', 'societas', and 'participatio'.

As one looks at the overall picture that Sagovsky provides, 'communion' emerges not as an untouchable metaphysical reality given a long time ago to the Church which history has irreparably destroyed whenever we started disagreeing with one another – whether about the doctrine of the Trinity in the fourth and fifth centuries, the Eucharist in the sixteenth, or gender and sexuality in the late twentieth and early twenty-first. It is rather a paradoxical reality, a mark of the divine gift of new life to the Church, which nonetheless exists in flesh and blood, and with which the Church has to struggle as we move through every epoch of human history – which is also God's history, because it is the continuation of salvation-history. Sagovsky must have had both his acute historical perspective and today's 'unhappy divisions' in mind when he wrote this somewhat telling observation towards the end of his book:

It is a matter of faith, that when debates become dead-locked, in the very activity of mutual dialogue there will emerge a deeper and more truthful *koinonia*. Here we have to argue against the premature foreclosing of debates, against comfortable *koinonia* (the ecclesiastical equivalent of 'the neighbourhood watch'), the illegiti-mate manufacture and imposition of consensus that is ultimately a failure of faith in God the Holy Spirit to lead God's people through the wilderness into all truth.[3]

Here, Sagovsky makes two vital points, with something of a two-edged sword. On the one hand, he tells us with all the compelling gentleness of history that 'we have been here before': not in the sense of having encountered today's problems in a preceding century which we have conveniently forgotten, but in the sense of having experienced harsh disagreements that are the hallmarks of church history – which we ignore at our peril. The Acts of the Apostles, frequently held up as a tale of inevitable church growth, is also an account of struggle in the face of persecution, and an ongoing disagreement about circumcision which we in our age find it almost impossible to understand, yet which threatened to divide irreparably the fledgling Christian mission.

The other point Sagovsky is making is about foreclosing debate through the imposition of a premature (and inadequate) agreement before those involved are really ready for it. History will tell us again and again, both negatively and positively, how important it is not just to dialogue about differences, but to locate where the disagreement actually exists – where lies real potential for lasting agreement, if not willing sympathy. Nicholas Thompson has recently shown how in the opening years of the Reformation, the area of eucharistic sacrifice (perhaps fortunately, unlike eucharistic presence, never conciliarly defined by the medieval Church) was on the receiving end of some potentially fruitful agreement, thanks to the work of Martin Bucer on the Reformation side, and Johannes Gropper on the Catholic.[4] But it was not to be. It has been left to more recent history to try to work at fresher forms of agreement

through ecumenical dialogue. What Sagovsky is saying to
us is that history is perhaps too full of missed opportunities,
and one of the lessons we can learn is not to repeat old
mistakes when facing new problems.

It is, nonetheless, one thing to look at the past with a new
insight on a word like 'communion'. It is altogether a different exercise to engage in the flesh and blood of heated
controversy. And the trouble with the past (apart from the
fact that it is always, at least partially, over!) is that what
bothered people then has the habit of not producing quite
so much hot temper today. But the same three 'Views' keep
persisting. All well and good, but what exactly can we say
about the more restrictive aspect of 'communion'?

A Theology of Limits

For some years, I used to teach the history of Christian
liturgy, which was usually based on set texts. One of these
was the (so-called) 'Apostolic Tradition', which a previous
generation thought was the work of the third-century
theologian, Hippolytus of Rome, and which has been used
as the basis for much of the rewriting of liturgical texts as a
result. (Since that time, the identification with Hippolytus
has been discredited, leaving one with an historical irony,
that the document seems to have had more influence on the
twentieth century than on the fourth and fifth.) In the
sample eucharistic prayer suggested for use at an episcopal
ordination, there is one expression whose meaning no one
has managed to fathom. It comes in the thanksgiving series,
just before the narrative of the Last Supper: 'when he was
being handed over to voluntary suffering, that he might
destroy death and break the bonds of the devil, and tread
down hell and illuminate the righteous, *and fix a limit* and

manifest the resurrection'.[5] As Bradshaw, Johnson, and Phillips note in their commentary, there are a number of different interpretations, such as the limit of hell, or the resurrection, or more generally of doctrine. It seems a strange word to use, whatever its meaning, at this particular point, and it is worth noting that modern prayers inspired by this source (of which there are many) studiously avoid even trying to reproduce a parallel to this tantalising image.

Whatever its precise meaning, the fact remains that something about limits occurred to someone, somewhere, as an appropriate image to include in the heart of the eucharistic prayer. Of course, God knows no limits, and if he did, he would not be God. But we who exist in space and time are only too aware of our own limitations, which define who we are, what we are experiencing, and what we hope to do and to be in the future. We are thus faced with a yawning gap – between ourselves, and our own limitations, and the God we love and worship, who is beyond space and time. But we also have to face the fact that, in some sense, Christ does 'fix a limit', a boundary, which is as much about what we are saved from as about how much we are able to put into words. Paul's hymn to love in his First Letter to the Corinthians posits the Christian community both in history and on the verge of eternity when he says: 'Now I know only in part; then I will know fully, even as I have been fully known' (1 Corinthians 13:12b).

That leaves us with the challenge of both accepting the provisionality of all that we are, and of having to be part of a community with its own disciplines, its own norms for worship, its own style of conducting public discourse, all of which express, implicitly or explicitly, our destiny in God. This is what we mean by the Catholic Church, whose existence we profess in the Creeds. Contrary to what we are

sometimes told, the overall impression one gets from
reading the New Testament is not one of unalloyed glad-
ness in being a member of the Body of Christ. It is not easy,
or straightforward, or without cost. When Jesus tells us to
take up our cross daily and follow him (Luke 9:23), that
cross will be as much about our differences with one
another as it will concern our own inward struggles, such as
with serious illness, and the hostility that following Christ
sometimes means.

Paul wrote one of his most magnificent passages, about
love, because it was wrung out of him by the heart-breaking
cliqueiness of Corinth, and the religious fad of placing
certain other gifts, like speaking in tongues, in a class above
all others. One of the most fruitful areas of biblical studies
in our time is how we are more aware of the history of
interpretation. Scripture emerges as a rich pool in which to
bathe, rather than a rigid conceptual framework from which
to write off specific propositions that are in some way
logically vindicated for ever. It is obvious that, for example,
Anglicanism is far stronger, numerically, in Africa, than it is
in Europe. But Europe's own sad history of *not* dealing with
difficulty and disagreement, and its legacy of schism and
splits when all was not yet lost, should provide a strong
caution against a false religious zeal that makes the added
mistake of thinking that history is always, in some way,
'inevitable'. There are times to lay down the theological
weapons in the conceptual armoury – and try both to speak
and live the peace that passes all understanding.

In practical terms, however, there are 'limits' set out in
the *Windsor Report*.[6] It is widely regarded as an important
step in providing some sort of 'ground rules' for dealing
with major points of dispute in a world-wide Church that
neither has nor wants some kind of central magisterium.

History will tell whether it will turn out to be – in the long term – an attempt to foreclose a wider and longer debate. Its observations are both shrewd and generous. But is its understanding of 'covenant' too hasty? It helps us to clarify Anglican 'Instruments of Unity', and the way in which each is circumscribed, whether in the role of the Archbishop of Canterbury, the Lambeth Conference, the Anglican Consultative Council, or the Primates' Meetings. It is important, too, that they are seen in the wider historical context of the conciliar movement in the later Middle Ages as well as modern ecumenical theology, as Paul Avis has recently shown.[7] But there is a creeping sense of an 'either-or' when confronting the issues of the day, as if tradition were something more static than history reveals it to be, and that to push at the boundaries of accepted norms (whether in theology or ethics) must always lead to cultural relativism. And for certain Primates to refuse to receive communion with the Archbishop of Canterbury, for whatever reason, is for many of us (at best) somewhat puzzling behaviour, or (at worst) an action that seriously undermines their own position, if not also their collective trustworthiness.

There is indeed a series of problems, some of which are arguably more cultural than theological. As part of the celebration of the 200th anniversary of the passing of the law against trading in slavery, I had to preach during Choral Evensong from Portsmouth Cathedral, on BBC Radio 3. Throughout the service, and the other events and broadcasts through that week during March 2007, I became more and more aware how much of a legacy the slave trade has left behind, in memories that need to be healed, and in mutual antagonisms, between Great Britain, West Africa, the West Indies, and North America. Although slavery had long been practised in Africa before the British arrived, it was the scale of our exploitation of this disgraceful trade in human beings that is so reprehensible. Too often social and cultural reasons for potentially church-dividing areas are swept aside as 'clouding the issue'. But my own experience of the Anglican Communion leads me to think that those reasons loom far more largely, widely, and deeply than many of us realise. They certainly played a critical role in the creation of some of the schisms in the Christian East, for example with the (Syriac-speaking) so-called Nestorian Church as long ago as the fifth century.

I have sometimes observed at meetings with fellow-bishops that we tend to rush into talking about ecclesiology, because it has something to do with being a bishop!; perhaps we should find ourselves talking about anthropology instead. My own experience of fighting serious illness has repeatedly brought me face to face with the centrality of the doctrine of God and the human race (my humanity included!) in a sharper way than ever before, the Church taking very much second place. Jesus came to save the world, after all, and the founding of the Church only came along as a consequence of that central, salvific act. This does not mean some kind of free-for-all, of which Anglicans are often accused, not without justification. But it is an argument for accepting that, just as there are different ways of 'reading Scripture' across the centuries and cultures, so there must be some degree of concomitant pressure in the way we order our lives as Christians. Catholicity is about universality – but it is in denial of reality when it presents itself in static terms. There is a dynamic of tradition that is always going to create rough edges, where boundaries are pushed at and risks taken, in the belief that this is the (sometimes untidy) way in which the Spirit speaks to the Churches.

Three Observations

First of all, a practical observation. The *Windsor Report* rightly focuses on the 'Instruments of Unity'. But it suggests that we need much more. The notion of an Anglican Covenant has much to commend it, but there is always a fear and a suspicion that it will be used in order to 'police' the Communion. To take examples from contemporary controversies, North America is chastised for some of its decisions and the way that these were taken, but what happens if the same kind of umbrage is visited on Nigeria, for rewriting its constitution in a way further to the theological 'right' than it was before, in order to send clear signals to those who do not concur? What we badly need are more bilateral (and even trilateral, as James Jones has shown) links between dioceses and Provinces. Some of the other contributions among these essays tell their own tale of mutual understanding and openness of dialogue that provide a far more vibrant picture of the Anglican Communion as it works on the ground than is often portrayed in public discussion and media comment.

Our West African Link in Portsmouth, which now concentrates on Ghana but still involves parts of Nigeria, has convinced me over the years that this is where our real strength lies. Bilateral is nearly always enriched by a third party, and here we bring our equally cherished link (through the Porvoo Agreement) with the Lutheran diocese of Stockholm, and its bishop, Caroline Crook. I recall introducing her to two Nigerian bishops who were visiting us in Portsmouth as part of our 75th anniversary celebrations as a diocese. For every one in that room (except myself) it was their first meeting with a bishop who was a woman, and the roof did not fall in; nor did the heavens open with rain when we all appeared, fully robed, at the outdoor Eucharist on the following Sunday. In a globalised world, personal contacts and friendships of this kind are at a premium, and they can achieve far more than official pronouncements from the hierarchy. Part of the price we pay for not having a central authority – which few of us want – is that we need to resource and value these encounters.

Secondly, an ecclesiological observation. We need to loosen up (I would almost say 'lighten up'!) on the way we write about the Church, which at times can seem heavy, pompous, and self-regarding. In a recent article, the Romanian Orthodox scholar, John McGuckin has written about the ecclesiology of the third-century Alexandrian theologian Origen.[8] Towards the end, McGuckin treads less warily when he draws a contrast between Cyprian, whom we tend to regard as thoroughly sound, and Origen himself, who for all his brilliance has still enjoyed a somewhat checkered history, because of his views on good and evil, and some of the ways he interprets Scripture.

For McGuckin, however, Cyprian and Origen (North Africans, albeit from different parts, that they both were!), represent different approaches to what the Church is. Cyprian's ecclesiology appears at times to be rigid and anxious, no doubt the result of the context in which he lived, and his calling in the Church as bishop of a persecuted flock. Useful at a time of crisis, McGuckin maintains, it cannot be the last word. As a Church, we do tend nowadays to go further than Origen and appear both angst-ridden and brittle, because perhaps we feel embattled and think that it all depends on us (which it does not!). For all the difficulties he experienced in his own time, he persisted in the belief that all humans are called, potentially, to be part of the Church by the God who stoops to come to earth in order to teach us in the ways of truth, virtue, and hope, the ways of healing and striving for perfection.

Thirdly, a theological observation. On Easter Eve, 2007, two religious articles appeared in the *Guardian* newspaper. As a daily, it is not known for pandering to religiosity. But it does have a reputation for greater seriousness in handling religious matters than the other mainstream papers. In the 'Face to Faith' column, which appears every Saturday, there was a short, snappy, and engaging piece by Tom Wright, the Bishop of Durham. It was vintage stuff, biblically based, counter-cultural, and with an underlying message that was evangelical in scope: forget about the Easter trappings, just read the gospel narratives, and see what happens. Three pages earlier, there was a more discursive piece by Giles Fraser, Rector of Putney, a regular contributor who is apt to take conservatives and evangelicals (preferably both!) to task. Of Jewish descent, he produced a piece about the importance of the Passover as a key to Easter, with its overall message of freedom; and towards the end he took a pot-shot at people in the Church who are obsessed with the errors of licence and the need for control. On the Monday edition, there appeared two letters condemning Fraser and voting for Wright, only to be followed by two further letters on the Tuesday which said how helpful Fraser had been! A reputable national paper with a track record of (sometimes not very thinly veiled) secularism not only gave space to two writers such as these, with their very different approaches, but then followed this up with mutually contradictory comments from four readers. Here was something central – the Easter message – given centre stage. It is important that theological debate should be held in public in this way, so that we can (when necessary) be exposed to the experience of being shamed by those who haven't a clue about what or who we are, and may even have some prophetic things to say to us from the outside about our priorities, and the way we can squander our energies on matters that future generations may well be aghast at.

Conclusion

I want to continue to be part of a Church which can embrace both those brilliant minds – and I have no intention of letting myself be pushed out by any religious-political thought-police in consequence. Nor do I want episcopacy to become so consumerised that it is only possible to work with people with whom one agrees on absolutely everything: that would be a denial of catholicity, and set dangerous precedents for the next time we start falling out with each other. Instead of a covenant, we need patience – patience to work at disagreements rather than superimposing a methodology of agreement in advance. A schism, after all, arising from ethical tensions is bound to result in the worst kind of censoriousness.

If communion has ever been impaired, it did not begin when Anglicans started to disagree about ethical or gender issues. Impaired communion – communion in conflict – began at the Last Supper, with the presence of the betrayer (Luke 22:21ff.) and the dispute among the disciples as to who was the greatest (Luke 22:24ff.). On that score, communion must always live the paradox of a divine originator – and very human participants. To revert yet again to the three approaches mentioned earlier, if we wait until everything is sorted out, we shall fragment into separate jurisdictions; if we federate into the likeminded, we shall lose out on breadth; but if we struggle on with the gift of

God in his communion and ours, we are more likely to become better witnesses to the Gospel of the cross in a broken and divided world.

Notes

1 See *InterCommunion: A Scottish Episcopalian Approach* (Edinburgh: Representative Church Council, 1969).
2 See Nicholas Sagovsky, *Ecumenism, Christian Origins and the Practice of Communion* (Cambridge: Cambridge University Press, 2000).
3 Ibid., p. 203.
4 See Nicholas Thompson, *Eucharistic Sacrifice and Patristic Tradition in the Theology of Martin Bucer 1534–1546* (Studies in the History of Christian Traditions CXIX) (Leiden: Brill, 2005).
5 See Paul F. Bradshaw, Maxwell E. Johnson, L. Edward Phillips (eds), *The Apostolic Tradition* (Hermeneia Series) (Minneapolis: Fortress Press, 2002), p. 40 (text), pp. 47–48 (commentary).
6 See *The Lambeth Commission on Communion: The Windsor Report 2004* (London: Anglican Communion Office, 2004).
7 See Paul Avis, *Beyond the Reformation? Authority, Primacy and Unity in the Conciliar Tradition* (London: Continuum, 2006); I am much indebted to this important work, an example of historical theology at its most informative.
8 See John A. McGuckin, 'Origen of Alexandria and the Mystery of the Pre-existent Church', in *International Journal for the Study of the Christian Church* 6.3 (2006), 207–222.